*f***P**

What KiDS Buy and Why

The PSYCHOLOGY
of MARKETING to KIDS

DAN S. ACUFF, Ph.D

with Robert H. Reiher, Ph.D

THE FREE PRESS
New York   London   Toronto   Sydney   Singapore

*f*P

THE FREE PRESS
A Division of Simon & Schuster Inc.
1230 Avenues of the Americas
New York, NY 10020

Designed by Michael Mendelsohn of MM Design 2000, Inc.

Manufactured in the United States of America

10 9 8 7 6 5 4 3 2 1

Library of Congress Cataloging-in-Publication Data

Acuff, Dan S., 1942–
    What kids buy and why / Dan S. Acuff with Robert H. Reiher.
        p.   cm.
    ISBN 0–684–83448–0
    1. Child consumers.   2. New products.   3. Child development.
    4. Cognition in children.   I. Reiher, Robert H.   II. Title.
    HF5415.32.A25   1997
    658.8'34'083—dc21
                                                    97–33491
                                                        CIP

To the preciousness and sacredness
of the hearts and minds of children everywhere.
May we always strive to earn their trust.

Contents

INTRODUCTION

ince 1989 the birth rate of children in the United States alone has jumped from approximately 3.5 million a year to over 4 million, maintaining a "baby-boom" pace into the mid 1990s. This, along with a variety of socio-cultural changes, translates to direct-purchase and purchase-influence "kid power" that exceeds $200 billion a year.

This kid-buying power is increasing. With societal changes such as those brought on by the substantial shift from mothers working at home to mothers working outside the home, and the increase in single-parent families, children have had to take on more responsibility. This includes much more direct-purchasing activity for themselves and their families as well as substantially more influence when it comes to which restaurants and fast-food outlets to frequent, which pizza to order, which groceries and home necessities to buy, which computer systems, which brands of clothing—even which type of automobile to buy for the family.

Kids have never before wielded the purchase power that they wield today. Dr. James McNeal, in his book *Kids as Customers,* has even coined the term *filiarchy* to describe the burgeoning potency of today's young people in the marketplace.[1]

With so much direct purchase power at stake it is critical to understand just who these kids are. In recent years a variety of entities have entered the scene with the intent of educating corporate America and other interested individuals about "kids"—about what's motivating them, their preferences, their differences by gender and age, the latest kid and youth trends. Whereas a few years ago there were no conferences on product development on marketing to kids, now there are a variety of these conferences each year attended by hundreds and organized and presented by groups including the International Quality and Productivity Center,[2] the Institute for International Research,[3] and the *Marketing to Kids Report.*[4] There are also two periodicals which cover kids as consumers and effective approaches to marketing to them: the *Marketing to Kids Report* just cited, and *Selling to Kids.*[5]

People targeting kids are thirsty for more knowledge about today's young people. What are the success stories in marketing to kids and their parents? Why have many kid-targeted products and programs failed? Most important, what are the inner workings of today's kids as to their preferences, their tastes, their purchasing behavior? Essential insights into these inner workings—the psychological underpinnings of kids and their motivations, interests, and behavior—form the central focus of this book.

WKB is a guide to the successful creation, development, and marketing of products and programs targeted to today's youth ages birth through the teen years. "Products" include virtually anything targeted for sale to kids, such as toys, games, sporting goods, foods, software, publications, clothing, and such personal hygiene items as shampoo or toothpaste. "Programs" include such entertainment programming as feature films, TV animation, and electronic games, and such "edutainment" as educational software. In Chapter 1, we look at what it takes to be a winner among the proliferation of products and programs aimed at today's youth.

Chapter 2 raises the issue of "kid empowerment." Beyond what "wins" at the cash registers or the box office, which products and programs contribute to the positive growth and development of children, and which may actually result in a negative impact? It's very important to get our priorities straight in terms of what's good and bad for kids as we develop and launch kid-targeted products and programs. While this book will facilitate the successful creation, development, and marketing of *any* product or program targeted to kids, our goal is to encourage and promote the development of products and programs that *empower*—that is, those that advance the *positive* development and growth of children and young people.

Chapter 3 presents a step-by-step guide to the successful development of kid-targeted products and programs. One by one, the important considerations and steps necessary in order to maximize one's chances for success are detailed.

Special attention throughout *WKB* is paid to age segmentation and targeting. The key differences, for example, between 3-through-7-year-olds and 8-through-12-year-olds and other "age segments" will be explored thoroughly in Chapters 4 through 8. What are the differences in children's neurological or brain development? What is going on with each age child socially? Emotionally? Morally? How do they perceive verbal and visual information at different ages and stages of development? What types of humor appeal to young people at what ages? How must gender differences be taken into account along the product- and program-development path, as children move through these developmental stages? What are the key implications of all this information for successful product and program development and marketing?

In Chapter 9, entitled "Barbie® Meets Godzilla®," gender differences are presented in detail along with numerous examples. In Chapter 10,

"Kids and Characters," the appeal of and effective use of cartoon-like characters and sports and entertainment personalities is examined. In Chapter 11 the arena of kid marketing is explored, including insights into effective youth-targeted naming, packaging, promotions, and advertising. Finally, Chapter 12 sums up what we have learned.

WKB is intended for a wide range of readers. Whether you are charged with new product or program creation, development, or marketing in the corporate world in America or abroad; whether you are an independent developer, an educator, or a parent, access to the information and insights provided in *WKB* will greatly assist you. Statistics show that in most product and program categories as many as 80 percent of new ideas outright fail, or at best fall short of meeting company expectations in the kids marketplace. While there is no insurance policy that will magically guarantee your success, what *will* make the difference in turning this statistic in your favor is an in-depth working knowledge of and insight into the inner life of the child as the consumer and user of your products and programs.

CHAPTER 1

A WINNING FORMULA

What do Barbie®, Garfield, Hi-Ho! Cherry-O, He-Man, See-N-Say, Tasmanian Devil, Cabbage Patch Kids, SpaghettiOs, Power Rangers, *Animaniacs, Ghostbusters, Star Wars,* Hot Wheels cars, Mario Brothers, UNO, Winnie the Pooh, Carmen Sandiego, Mickey Mouse, Spider-Man, Colorforms, LEGO, GIJoe, *Home Alone,* X-Men, Pound Puppies, *Jurassic Park,* Jim Carrey, Pop Tarts, Math Blaster, Reader Rabbit, Bugs Bunny, M&M's candies, *The Ren & Stimpy Show,* Nike shoes, the Big Mac, Sonic the Hedgehog, Froot Loops, Fruit Roll-Ups, *E.T.,* Batman, *The Lion King,* the Frisbee, Gak, *Hercules,* the Tickle Me Elmo doll, and the Little Caesar's pizza commercials have in common?

They are winners with kids.

Many of them are megawinners. Barbie® alone consistently accounts for over $1 billion in gross annual revenues for Mattel Incorporated.

For every winner there are scores of losers and underachievers—products and programs that either outright fail or do not live up to their projected expectations in the marketplace. In some industries, the success rate of new product and program introductions is as low as 20 percent. What is it about this winning 20 percent? What do winning products and programs have in common? Is there a "winning formula" that will *guarantee* success?

No. As in life itself, there are no guarantees.

There is, however, an approach to product and program development and marketing that will maximize opportunity for success. If a 20 percent success rate can be elevated to a 30 percent success rate, or to 40 percent, it would have a seismic impact on a company's bottom-line profits. What is that approach? It is a thorough and *integrated* approach to product and program development that has *knowing the targeted consumer* at the core—knowing his/her brain development, needs, motivations, and wants, and the way he/she perceives the world. We call this approach Youth Market

Systems, because over the past fifteen years of consulting on winning products and programs such as Barbie, He-Man, the Cabbage Patch Kids, Winnie the Pooh, Reader Rabbit, and Chuck E. Cheese's, we have been able to *systematize* what we have learned "in the trenches" with companies targeting kids. Most central to this systematic approach is a deep and profound understanding of the underlying abilities, motivations, needs, and behaviors of the young target. Providing a deep and clear understanding of this young consumer is the core emphasis of this book. If there ever were to be a winning formula for success for the youth marketplace, it would be "Know Thy Kid!"

THE PRODUCT LEVERAGE MATRIX

Winning kid-targeted products or programs such as Trix cereal, *Where in the World Is Carmen Sandiego?,* Sonic the Hedgehog, and the UNO card game have what might be termed "leverage" with kids. Leverage essentially translates as "power"—that is, the character, product, or program not only catches the attention of the targeted child consumer but meets his needs at a substantial level. It's critical to note that what provides this power with each product or program differs substantially. The Product Leverage Matrix illustrated below is a fundamental tool for getting at where the power is (or isn't) within a given product or program, and is a comprehensive model for either the analysis of an existing product or program or the development of a new one. The Product Leverage Matrix, which follows, is so fundamental to successful product and program development that it is used as a working tool repeatedly throughout this book.

This Product Leverage Matrix represents an integration of and a condensation of years of research and practical application. This tool helps us see the big picture and keeps in front of us what we need to know and to ask in order to *integrate* all aspects of a product or program. The variables that appear on the Product Leverage Matrix are detailed as follows:

MEDIUM/PRODUCTS: What is the medium, format, or product category? For example, is it a book, a video game, a TV show, a fast-food outlet, a toy? Are we dealing with product packaging? Is our focus on a spokescharacter such as Tony the Tiger?

Examples: Star Wars is a movie, a toy line, a book series, and a license for clothing, video games, foods, and fast foods among others, whereas Frisbees are primarily toys or sports equipment.

CONCEPT: What is the core idea of the product or program?

FIGURE 1.1: THE PRODUCT LEVERAGE MATRIX

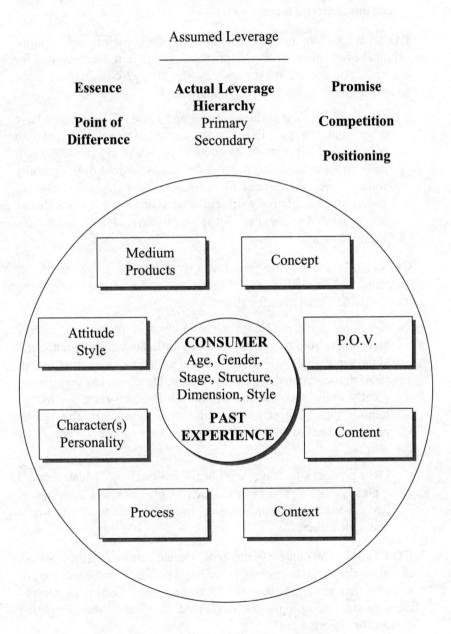

Assumed Leverage

Essence

Point of
Difference

Actual Leverage
Hierarchy
Primary
Secondary

Promise

Competition

Positioning

Medium
Products

Concept

Attitude
Style

CONSUMER
Age, Gender,
Stage, Structure,
Dimension, Style
PAST
EXPERIENCE

P.O.V.

Character(s)
Personality

Content

Process

Context

Example: The Cabbage Patch Kids concept was extremely successful in utilizing the core idea, or concept, of adopting orphans. Pound Puppies came along a short time later and also capitalized on this powerful theme.

P.O.V.: What is the product or program's psychological and/or philosophical orientation, or P.O.V. (point of view)? Is it conservative, for example? Antisocial? What is its message, if any? What impact might any of this have on the company's image?

Example: The Ren & Stimpy Show and some MTV cartoons have a definitely "edgy" P.O.V., with many references to snot and boogers and other gross anatomical objects and events. A company considering using them under license would most certainly want to take this potentially controversial P.O.V. into account. Even though a relatively straightforward product such as a cheese snack targeted to kids may not appear to have a P.O.V., it does: it's straightforward.

CONTENT: What is the Verbal or Visual content of the product or program? This is really a way of breaking out the central concept into its verbal and visual manifestations.

Examples: Sonic the Hedgehog has a visual "look" and an attitude/style that is both cute in his cartoony-little-animal appearance and at the same time is visually displayed as having an aggressive attitude. Sonic's appealing Visual content, therefore, has contributed greatly to his success. The *Winnie the Pooh* characters—Winnie himself, Piglet, Tigger, Eeyore—all have unique voices. This Verbal-content aspect of *Winnie the Pooh* has been an integral part of its success.

On a product's package, e.g., McDonald's Happy Meal, there is typically both Visual content, such as graphics and drawings of Ronald McDonald and his gang, and Verbal content—the words that appear there.

CONTEXT: The context is the geographical setting and time period, as well as the social ambience, i.e., what is going on in the social environment that surrounds the product or program? Also, what competitive products or programs exist? That is, what is the competing Context or environment?

Examples: The world or Context of Barbie® is that of today's teenager and post-teenager in America. This realistic, activity/fun-

and social-based context is integral to how young girls relate to her and identify with her. The Cabbage Patch Kids were born and raised in a cabbage patch. This extremely unusual and creative Context contributed greatly to their Point of Difference and set them apart from competing concepts. (Actually, the idea of the cabbage patch as a birthplace comes from European folklore— just as "the Stork" does.)

Context also refers to the time period in which the Concept takes place. It may be an Old West theme, for example, which takes place in the past, or a present-day sitcom, or a *Star Wars* future context. It may be also be a combination, e.g., the present/past– based *Jurassic Park.*

PROCESS: In essence, Process refers to the product/user interface. How does the product or program work? How does it involve the child? Is it fast or slow-paced? Does it use special effects? Music? Is it inter- active? Does the consumer read it? Watch it? Play with it? In what way?

Examples: Different candies and kid-targeted foods can employ different processes. M&M's candies are unique in their smallness and design such that they are a colorful and unique eating experi- ence for kids. Pez candies involve the unique process of candy dis- pensing. DunkAroos involve the process of dipping a cookie-like snack into a frosting-like substance. Innovative processes are fun- damental to the success of new video games. Sonic the Hedge- hog's speed was a key process factor that provided something new and different for video game-playing kids. The movie *Star Wars* introduced a variety of innovative film processes, including break- through sound and visual effects. If a product or program devel- oper can provide their target with some unique and rewarding new Process, it may very well become a major success factor.

CHARACTER(S)/PERSONALITY: What fantasy-based or reality- based characters (if any) appear in or are used with the product or pro- gram? What are their archetypes? How does the targeted consumer identify with the characters? What are the dynamics and relationships between the characters?

Examples: Given that kids and characters seem to be inseparably joined at the hip, examples of characters that contribute toward a product or program's success abound: the Trix rabbit, *Batman, Barbie*®, *Mickey Mouse,* the *Animaniacs* characters, *Barney & Friends,* etc., etc.—at least a hundred characters could be named.

Among the most successful characters of all time are Bugs Bunny and Garfield. These characters also have a very broad range of appeal across many age segments—even for adults—because of their unique "looks," personalities, and behaviors. It's no accident that each of these characters has a "dark side" to it, e.g., Bugs Bunny with his acerbic wit, craftiness, and sarcasm, and Garfield with his aggressive abusiveness, indolence, and other self-serving traits. You'll find an in-depth look at kids and characters in Chapter 9.

ATTITUDE/STYLE: What is the product or program's Style and/or Attitude? For example, is it old-fashioned, futuristic, modern, country? Where graphics are concerned, are they plain? Abstract? Straightforward? Funky? Cool? What impact might this Attitude/Style have on the company's image?

Examples: Nike shoes and other apparel have exemplified innovative graphic design and style—to the point where the Nike logo alone carries a tremendous power of appeal. X-Men comics and action figures always carry a high-action, aggressive, colorful, in-motion Attitude/Style that appeals strongly to their male targets.

TOP OF MATRIX

There are other product-development, product-maximization, and marketing-related variables that appear at the top of the Product Leverage Matrix; these are important to take into consideration as well.

ESSENCE: This is an exercise that has proven very useful in the development and marketing stages of a product or program. *Essence* is the core idea of the product or program, and the exercise is to boil the concept down to as few words as possible. Getting at the core essence of a product or program assists greatly in maintaining focus on its key attributes throughout the product-development and marketing cycle.

Examples: Bugs Bunny = Clever cartoon rabbit
Kellogg's Pop Tarts = Fruit-flavored toaster pastries

POINT OF DIFFERENCE: What's different or unique about your product or program in relationship to competitive products or programs already in the marketplace? Without a potent or meaningful "point of difference" your product will not separate itself sufficiently. Also, it's very important to consider: *Is your point of difference a point* *of difference that really makes a difference?* In other words, is it powerful in the perception of your targeted consumer? So what if your gizmo is bigger and greener than the competition's? Is this difference really impactful?

Example: Where in the World Is Carmen Sandiego? separated itself from competitive learning-software games in several ways:

a. A female yet dark (villainess/criminal) central Character
b. The Content mix of linking learning (geography) with a fun game
c. The unique Process of how the game is played, searching the world for Carmen Sandiego

ASSUMED LEVERAGE VS. ACTUAL LEVERAGE: Typically in the product-development cycle, there are some assumptions made about what the Leverage or power of a concept is. We refer to these assumptions as the Assumed Leverage.

Example: If a new competitor to the Gatorade/Powerāde category—let's call it Enerjuice—is being developed with teens as the primary target, a set of assumptions might include:

a. Teens want more energy.
b. Teens identify with hero athletes.
c. Teens want great taste.
d. Teens will like the new product name: Enerjuice.

Assumptions are also made regarding the hierarchy, or relative power of each of these assumptions in relation to one another.

What's important to note here is that more often than not these assumptions are left unexamined as to veracity and strength. It's an important practice to check assumptions: check what the leverage *actually* is, and its relative power versus what has been *assumed.* More often than not, adults make erroneous assumptions about what kids perceive to be important and powerful because adults are looking at their product or program through adult eyes. It is critical to get at the actual leverage rather than the assumed leverage. With the above hypothetical Enerjuice example in mind, adults may be surprised when testing directly with kids' focus groups reveals that the new product's blue color is its most powerful point of leverage and that the majority of kids tested dislike the new name.

Direct kid-and-parent testing is fundamental to making sure that what is being assumed as having "leverage" or being powerful actually is. At Youth Market Systems (YMS) Consulting we have designed what we call "Subject Testing," which is a more experimental design approach: we study the concept to be tested first via the YMS systems models, then come up with hypotheses about how kids or parents are going to respond, *then* test to confirm or refute these hypotheses.

PROMISE: This Promise variable assists us in getting at the actual power or impact that a product or program has. The question is straightforward: What does the product promise the consumer/user? What key benefits does it provide? And how impactful and important are those benefits to the purchaser/consumer?

> *Example:* If I am a snack-food company and I am considering using Jim Carrey's *Mask* character under license on my product line, what does this *Mask* character promise the consumer? Possible responses: Outrageous fun, a weird visual "look," bizarre behavior that involves the consumer. At a deeper, more psychological level, one might say that Jim Carrey's *Mask* character allows the unexpressed "dark side" of consumers to find vicarious expression. Often it is such "looking beneath the surface" of what is attracting kid consumers that will reveal strong keys to what a product, program, or character is promising.

COMPETITION: It is very important to know what already exists in the competitive environment and how your product or program separates itself from these competing products or programs. How does your Point of Difference stack up against theirs? A very useful exercise here is to ask yourself: How does the Actual Leverage of my product measure up against the Actual Leverage of my competition?

POSITIONING: *Positioning* refers to how you want the product or program to be positioned or categorized in the mind of the targeted consumer. Imagine that the mind is a series of "mail slots." Let's assume that you are developing a new toy action figure of the muscular He-Man variety, and that your target is 3-through-7-year-old males. How will these young boys "mail-slot" your new action figure? Will they say, "Wow! That's different—it swells to twice its size when you put it in water! No other action figure does that!"? Or will they say, "Oh, another muscle-man action figure, ho-hum . . ."?

> *Examples:* Positioning also refers to the use of a Positioning Line or Tag Line that goes with a product or program and supports the

positioning direction, e.g., "He-Man—The Strongest Man in the Universe!" or *Disney Adventures* magazine's positioning-line subtitle, *The Magazine for Kids.*

Many products and programs miss the opportunity to utilize a Positioning Line and others use less than impactful Lines. Powerfully positioning your product or program in the minds of your targeted customers/viewers is an important opportunity to announce key benefits of your product and it has the potential of increasing consumer attention and involvement significantly. At the same time, an effective Positioning Line aids you in staying close to the "essence" or core idea/benefit of your product or program throughout the product-development and marketing process, and this is critical to an effective marketing campaign.

THE BIG PICTURE

This is where the integrative nature of the Product Leverage Matrix comes into play. The Matrix is extremely useful for holding the whole picture or "big picture" in place as your focus is directed to individual aspects of a product or program. In the *Mask* example above, once the promise is determined, a company would be wise to check on other variables that would be important to consider. For example, what about the impact that Carrey's bizarreness might have on the company's image? The question of "image" is reflected in the P.O.V. and Attitude/Style variables on the Matrix. Other variables should be looked at as well.

Essence: Is the *Mask* license a match with the Essence of the product?
Gender: Will the *Mask* character result in male bias?
Regarding Content: Is there any objectionable Content inherent in associating *Mask* with my product?

The Product Leverage Matrix can be also utilized to analyze a winning product or program in order to arrive at its strengths. For example, for the perennially successful kid's cereal Trix we have a good-tasting, sweet and colorful cereal (*Content*) that is combined with a fun character (*Character*)—the Trix Rabbit—who is constantly and humorously being foiled in his attempts to get Trix for himself (*Content*). "Silly rabbit, Trix are for Kids!" is a positioning coup in itself. The Attitude/Style is bright, energetic, and colorful and the *Promise* is "a colorful cereal with a sweet, fruity taste that has a fun rabbit tied to it."

THE CENTER OF THE MATRIX

However critical it might be to understand and integrate all the variables of the Matrix that we have defined so far, none of it will matter much if the center of the Matrix is ignored or inaccurately taken into account. In fact, what separates this book from others on product development and marketing is its central focus and emphasis on the child as consumer.

AGE: What is the targeted age range? Is it 3 through 7? 4 through 12? 8 through 15? Can your product or program appeal across age breaks as they are set out and defined in this book: birth through 2, 3 through 7, 8 through 12, 13 through 15, and 16 through 19?

It's very important to note that we at YMS Consulting have based our approach to dividing kids into distinct age segments on in-depth research on a wide range of factors including the child's cognitive development and brain research such as that of Brazelton,[1] Epstein,[2] Erikson,[3] Gazzaniga,[4] Herman,[5] Kohlberg,[6] MacLean,[7] Pearce,[8] and Piaget,[9] and upon fifteen years of focus-group (subject-testing) experience with hundreds of children of various ages and stages of development. It is also important to note that there is no right or correct approach to dividing kids into age segments. There will always be some disagreement, as well as future research that may challenge the age segmentation boundaries. It is also important to state that children often vary in the pace of their individual development, in their forms and levels of intelligence, and in their learning styles. There will always be exceptions to the age segmentation boundaries—precocious or regressive individuals.

GENDER: Are you targeting both males and females? What differences between them do you need to take into account?

STAGE: What stage of development is your targeted-age child in? Is she in the 3-through-7 "Autonomy" stage, the 8-through-12 "Rule/Role" stage? What are the implications of this?

STRUCTURE: "Structure" refers to the predominant phase of brain development in which the targeted-age child finds himself. If he is 3 through 7 years old, then certain areas of the unfolding, developing brain play a major role in, for example, his thinking processes, his attraction to fantasy, and his inability to handle such abstract forms of thinking as logic, or the subtleties inherent in sarcasm. If, on the other hand, he is 13 through 15 years old, his mind includes a "formal operations" structure that can handle most forms of thinking, logic, and humor.

DIMENSION: A child's life can be thought of as occurring in a variety of dimensions. That is, the child experiences her life *physically, cognitively, emotionally, socially,* and *morally.*

STYLE: This refers to the "learning style" of the child. Some children are much more *visual* in their approach to learning and to the world. (Some people refer to this style as "right-brained"—although current research warns against a too simplistic approach to "right-" and "left-brain" categorizations.) Others are more *verbal* ("left-brained"). Some children respond best to a "hands-on" approach that involves touch and whole-body involvement (kinesthetic). It's interesting to note that each of these styles of learning correlate with Howard Gardner's dimensions of multiple intelligence.[10]

PAST EXPERIENCE: The past experience of the child is very important to take into consideration on a variety of fronts. What past experience has added to your target child's being predisposed—or not—toward your product/program? What past experience has your targeted child had with similar or competing products or programs?

THE NEEDS AND WANTS OF THE TARGET CHILD

All of the above aspects of the children or youths that you are targeting with your product or program contribute toward the formation of their *needs* and *wants.* Successful products and programs are those that satisfy their needs and wants in the short term (impulse) or in the long term. While a colorful and involving Trix cereal package with a maze on the back provides for short-term needs satisfaction, Mattel's Hot Wheels cars year after year continue to provide young boys with something they need and want—small, easily manipulable, colorful minicars that are fun and involving to play "cars" with (Vroom! Vroom!) and to accumulate and collect.

Accumulating vs. Collecting: Before the age of approximately 6, children are interested in *accumulating* lots of toys or other fun objects just for the sheer number and mass that this represents. As they shift toward the more left-brain dominant, 8-through-12 stage, they develop the cognitive capacity to differentiate more precisely. This leads to what we term more serious *collecting,* which involves more comparison of details, more involvement with and attention to detail. Marvel comic-book-character cards, for example, describe the characters' various attributes, special skills, and abilities. Before the age of approximately 6 the capacity to meaningfully relate to these details is not in place; after 6 these details become very important and an essential part of what provides fun and involvement with the product.

At the center of the Product Leverage Matrix is the most critical variable: *the consumer.* The central thrust of this book is to lead the reader toward an in-depth understanding of the inner workings of these young consumers. The chapters that immediately follow provide an in-depth look into the lives of birth-through-2-year-olds, 3-through-7s, 8-through-12s, 13-through-15s, and 16-through-19-year-olds. We have divided or segmented the youth target in this way in accordance with a wide variety of scientific research, such as that of Piaget,[11] Erikson,[12] and Kohlberg.[13] Essentially the "breaks" between each of these age segments is established (Pearce,[14] Wilber[15]) because the child's brain undergoes a growth spurt or other shift in development at each of these segment breaks.

It is an in-depth understanding of the child consumer that provides the only real access to approximating a "winning formula" for the development of products and programs that succeed with kids. Is a successful product all that matters, however? In the next chapter we focus on kid empowerment. Before diving into what works and doesn't work for kids at different ages and stages of development, let's look at a very important issue: what's good and bad for kids, and how can you tell the difference? Then in Chapter 3 we outline the YMS approach to developing a new product or program from scratch. Many readers may want to read Chapters 4 through 8 first and then come back to Chapters 2 and 3, having gained a deeper knowledge and insight into the inner workings of the successive age segments of kids.

CHAPTER 2

KID EMPOWERMENT

Some men wish evil and accomplish it. But most men,
when they work in that machine, just let it happen somewhere in the wheels. The fault is no decisive, villainous
knife, but the dull saw that is the routine mind.
                                        —Stephen Vincent Benet,
                                        John Brown's Body[1]

Before we launch into understanding the inner workings of the birth-
through-19-year-old, let's examine a critical issue—kid empowerment.
At Youth Market Systems Consulting and the Character Lab, we're not just
interested in what sells, we're not just interested in the bottom line. We're
also interested in assisting companies to develop and promote products
and programs that are good for kids, that empower them. And we're four-
square against products and programs that can be shown in any significant
way to be bad for kids, that disempower them.

When it comes to the care and protection and well-being of children,
our world's most precious resource, there is a special responsibility to provide them with products and programs that are at least neutral in any good
or bad impact they might have on them, and at best products that are positive in their impact. At the same time it is our responsibility to protect the
world's children from products and programs that can be shown to have
significant deleterious impact. As Benet indicated above, the greatest danger is not overt evil intent, but the failure of child-targeted product and
program creators, developers, marketers, and decision makers to stand up
and act on what they know to be true regarding products and programs
with the potential to damage children's bodies or minds.

When the pressure mounts to put something out in the marketplace
that has clear potential to cause negative impact, such as excessively
violent concepts, sexist concepts, stereotypical or prejudicial cultural or
gender role concepts, sexually suggestive concepts, and disrespectful,
unnecessarily gross concepts, all of us in the youth-product business have
a responsibility to extricate ourselves from the corporate, almighty-dollar-

driven cogs that might just let these aberrations happen and to take a stand against them.

But just what is empowering and what is disempowering? What can be shown clearly to be good for kids and bad for kids? This is a very controversial question. For our purposes we define "empowering" products or programs as *those which contribute in some significant way toward an individual's positive development.* Disempowering products or programs, therefore, are *those which have a significant negative impact on an individual's development.*

Products or programs that disempower are those, therefore, which detract in some substantial way from a child's positive development. The word "substantial" is important here. It is seldom that one can find a product or program that is 100 percent positive or negative in terms of empowerment or disempowerment. For example, it could be argued that aspects of Snow White are disempowering, e.g., Snow White as a female victim who needs to be rescued by a male prince. Conversely it could be argued that *aspects* of highly violent films—much more violent than the *Power Rangers* movies—may actually be empowering, e.g., a film with an ending in which our horrendous villain transforms, sees the error of his ways, and repents.

This is not a simple issue. It is not an easy question of black or white; there can be a good deal of gray in between. A product or program that most everyone might agree is pure empowerment may have some aspects of it that could be argued to be disempowering. For example, Jane Healy, in her provocative and important book, *Endangered Minds,*[2] brings *Sesame Street*—a very "sacred cow"—under the microscope of empowerment and finds aspects of it that could be disempowering. Importantly, she brings into question the show's fast-paced sight and sound bites, and an approach to learning letters that may very well be inimical to learning to read effectively. Dr. Healy says:

> [W]e now realize that empty word recognition is a meaningless exercise. Twenty years of throwing alphabet letters and dancing words at children is producing exactly what we might expect: students who, even after learning to read, lack the foundations for further progress; children who find reading "boring," who are satisfied with the superficial, who can't understand why meaning doesn't magically appear—like a visual effect—and who give up when it doesn't. (p. 226)

Does this mean that *Sesame Street* is 100 percent bad for kids and therefore disempowering? No, of course not. It delivers many positive

Content messages such as getting along with others, trying hard, "you-can-do-it" self-esteem messages and cultural-diversity and acceptance messages mixed in with learning segments. What it *does* mean is that instead of accepting a product or program carte blanche, we need to examine each of its different aspects and its ultimate impact on kids at different ages and stages of development and from different cultural subgroups.

Conversely, a program such as *Power Rangers,* which many feel is too violent, and therefore may be negatively impacting its child audience in this regard, may have other aspects in its Content that are empowering, such as messages extolling the benefits of cooperation and teamwork.

It's not black or white.

There is, if you will, a continuum of empowerment from those products which are extremely disempowering to those which are extremely empowering. Another way to say it is that there may be aspects of a program that are empowering and aspects that may be disempowering. One needs to discern which are which and make a judgment call on an individual child's "take-away" from experiencing that product or program. This means: What is that individual left with? How has he been impacted? Has he been empowered? Has he been disempowered? In what ways? To what degree?

How is it to be determined, then, whether aspects of a product or program are "empowering" or "disempowering"? The technical, scientific answer to this question is that only after a great deal of testing in controlled studies can it be objectively determined. (And even then the research methodology and its conclusions can be brought into question.) For example, does TV violence influence children's violent predispositions and behavior? This question has definitely been proven to be a solid "Yes" through hundreds of studies. The evidence is virtually incontestable at this point. But in the absence of these kinds of studies, must we throw up our hands and resort to pure subjectivity? The authors don't think so. As parents, as teachers, as product and program developers we need to continue to confront ourselves with this critical issue of empowerment. We have to use any information that is available and our own common sense in order to determine whether a given product or program might be substantially positive or negative in its impact on the development of kids. The very future of humankind is at stake.

Then there's the issue of moderation. Because highly sweetened foods such as candy and sugar-coated cereals are arguably "bad" for kids when eaten to excess, does this mean they are disempowering products? Again, the authors don't think so. It's a question of moderation and balance. It's a question of children learning to make the right choices under the watchful and concerned guidance of informed and aware parents and caretakers.

Finally there's the issue of what we at YMS call the "psycho-cultural environment." Let's compare two similar kids in two very different settings. Jay is a 9-year-old male who watches sixteen hours of violent TV shows a week in his living room in suburbia where he is surrounded by the antiviolence influences of a stable home, church, school, and his (for the most part) nonviolent peers. Monty, by contrast, is a 9-year-old inner-city youth who watches those same sixteen hours of violent TV shows in his crowded apartment, occasionally interrupted by real gunfire, or sirens in the street, or by a knock at the door from an older 'hood youth who has been pressuring him to join "the gang" and who's there to tell him that his best friend has just been shot. There is a huge difference between Monty's "psycho-cultural environment" and Jay's.

We got a phone call recently from an ad agency for a major toy client. The agency had done some number crunching and discovered that boys' action figures—the kind that come with punching power, karate kicking functions, and a host of knives, swords, guns, bludgeons, clubs, bombs, missiles, and weapons of all kinds—were very popular with inner-city youth. Is that a surprise to anyone? But the shocking part was that they wanted to know if we could help them take advantage of this strong inner-city interest and help them sell more of these action figures to our inner-city children. We adamantly declined. We could only shake our heads in disbelief and disgust. Where are these people thinking from? Obviously they are not thinking. They are coming solely from a bottom-line perspective with blinders on regarding the larger social ramifications. The dull saw of the routine mind churns forward.

You decide. In this sometimes all-too-subjective world, is there a place for censorship? We absolutely think so.

Do we always give kids what they want? Let's go to the extreme. If we put on pornographic TV programming after school, do you think children would watch it? We have no doubt that a great many would. Does this mean we *should* put it on the air—after all, "They want it"? Because older males prefer the most violent electronic games, does this mean we should provide them with ever-increasingly violent electronic-game programming?

Issues of censorship and the impact of products and programs on our children—despite the difficulty of determining what is empowering and disempowering—must continue to be dealt with by product and program developers, by advertisers, and in board rooms across corporate America and the world.

TWO CASES: EMPOWERMENT AND DISEMPOWERMENT

Let's look at two distinct concepts, one targeting primarily females and the other males.

THE CABBAGE PATCH KIDS

Do the Cabbage Patch Kids dolls empower children? Again, we are defining "empowering products and programs" as those which provide something that a child needs or otherwise can use to help him or her develop positively as a human being.

In the case of the Cabbage Patch Kids, our answer is definitively "Yes." Children 3 through 7 are able to act out natural nurturing behaviors in most types of doll play as well as to learn from role-playing Mommy or Daddy and all the social interactions that come along with doll play. The added aspects of adoption and personalization simply add more "ownership" or personal involvement to the experience of the child as well as possibly a deeper emotional "connection" with the dolls. Along these same lines it could be argued that, from a prosocial perspective, involving a 3-through-7-year-old with a mock adoption lays foundations for increased compassion, responsibility, and generosity as an adult. This is true "empowerment." One would be hard-pressed to find anything disempowering about the Cabbage Patch Kids concept.

THE POWER RANGERS

A second case in point is the *Power Rangers* TV show. After careful analysis it is our view that this show is overall disempowering due to the central characters' use of physical power: hitting, punching, martial-arts moves, and the use of weapons such as rockets and other projectiles shot at other characters to dominate one's enemies and to solve one's problems This concept clearly falls under the category of shows the likes of which have been tested and proven to influence aggressive, violent behavior in children.

As we have said, there *are* aspects of the *Power Rangers* TV shows that could be labeled empowering, e.g., messages that are anti-theft or anti-lying, and positive "messages" at the end of shows. But in the end, one must ask oneself: What is a young child's primary "take-away" after watching a *Power Rangers* show or series of shows? Is he or she more likely to take away the positive messages or more likely to practice karate kicks? Is there a *substantial* element of violence and use of physical force

present in the *Power Rangers* shows that may result in more disempowerment than empowerment of our children?

Our response is "Yes." There is simply too much definitive research on
the subject of violence on television, and its negative influence on our
youth. It's no longer a debate. Seeing violence encourages doing violence.
End of story.

In 1995 a major Canadian network pulled the *Power Rangers* television show off the air because of complaints that children were hurting each
other while practicing *Power Rangers*-style kick-boxing techniques on the
playground. Innocent fun? Or practice in violent resolutions to problems?

Does this mean we'd like to see all forms of violence stripped from all
forms of media? Are we in favor of complete and total censorship? No.

This is not a simple issue. In Japan, for, example, they have more violence on television than we have in the United States. In particular, many
of their cartoons show explicit violence—heads being chopped off, blood
spattering, etc.—and yet the Japanese have less of a societal problem with
crime and violence than we do (at least so far). Why? The consensus is that
it is a "psychocultural environment" issue; they have much tighter control
than we do over the ethics and actions of individuals through strong societal moral influences and close-knit family structures.

It is beyond the scope of this book to offer an in-depth analysis of this
whole issue of violence. Suffice it to say that the authors stand for a re-
duction in violence, even a limiting of violence to what could be called
"indirect" forms of violence versus "direct" forms. In the *Road Runner*
cartoons, for example, Wile E. Coyote gets his just deserts by his own hands
through his own faux pas. The Road Runner never lays a feather on him.

This empowerment issue is also an issue that must be dealt with by
looking at what age and stage of development we are considering. Our
position after considerable study of the issue is that children below the age
of 15 would be much more empowered and less disempowered if they were
exposed to far less violence (and overt sexuality) than they are today. After
this age (when all cognitive functions are ideally fully in place) our young
people will be in a better place to be able to discern values for themselves
and less susceptible to negative role-modeling and influence.

We, the authors, also stand for and recommend definite censorship of
disempowering concepts and content targeted to consumers below the age
of 15. And in this regard, it should be no surprise that we are in full support
of the "V-chip" technology or other future technology which allows adults
to block out what they have determined, after serious consideration, to be
programming disempowering to children.

Of course we also stand for the development of children's programming that is very entertaining without being disempowering. In fact, our

commitment is so strong in this area that we've established, under the leadership of Dr. Robert Reiher, Innertainment Productions, with the objective of creating and developing programming that is highly entertaining and empowering via positive values and messages which are "imbedded" in the storylines.

One such program, for example, is *The HOO*™, which is designed for TV animation and children's radio. This program has been designed to be extremely entertaining as we follow the antics of a "tribe" of little HOO-owl characters; these are unwise owls who are trying to "get smart," but who more often than not fall on their little HOO faces and learn from their mistakes. There is also a lot of fun word play in the character names: HOOpty-Do, its main character, and his HOO Buddies, Yoo-HOO, Boo-HOO, and HOO-Ray. For purposes of empowerment, *The HOO*™ has the central theme of "helping children make better choices in life."

At Innertainment Productions we currently have a variety of children's positive programming concepts in development based upon developmentally sound empowerment strategies, such as:

A. Helping kids deal with their feelings more effectively
B. Helping them solve their personal problems
C. Increasing their positive self-concept and self-esteem
D. Helping them to listen better and pay better attention

OTHER MEDIUMS

Most of the examples cited above, e.g., the Cabbage Patch Kids, the Power Rangers, and *The HOO*™ are from the toy and children's animation arenas. Let's turn our empowerment-versus-disempowerment discussion toward other product and program categories.

ELECTRONIC GAMES: Unlike the copious research on television, insufficient research has been done on the effects of violence in dedicated-system or computer-based video games. Yet the similarities and parallels of the video-game medium to the television medium are so strong that one could easily extrapolate that excessively violent electronic games are indeed disempowering for kids.

There are also sexual/gender role issues that come into question. The portrayal of bosomy, scantily-clad female warriors is common in many action/fighting games. What does the child "take away" from these overt sexual images? In addition, when program developers have attempted to design programming directly and exclusively for the female audience, they have often fallen into the trap of portraying girls as sexual stereotypes—as shallow, vain, boy crazy, and interested only in boys and shopping. Computer programming (learning software) must also beware of this trap.

TV ADVERTISING: Care must be taken in advertising to avoid gender and cultural stereotypes. In addition, many TV ads show adults in rigid, unflattering, or demeaning roles—e.g., students shown to be superior in some way at the expense of their teacher, who is made out to be a fool. Just because kids like this kind of advertising and respond positively to it doesn't mean it should be presented on the air.

FEATURE FILMS: Feature films targeting kids and whole families should also be aware of cultural and gender stereotyping. While we are not suggesting that film developers, writers, and producers unrealistically change the roles of males or females or individuals from different races, we are suggesting that a sensitivity toward these roles be brought to bear along with a spirit of innovation—looking for ways to represent males, females, and individuals from different cultures in new and positive roles.

PACKAGING: Most packaging is rather innocuous and devoid of issues that could relate to what's good or bad for kids. Packaging that displays excessively violent and/or inappropriate sexual images and gender roles, however, such as can be found in the electronic-game sections of stores, is certainly open to criticism in those terms.

PROMOTIONS/LICENSING/TIE-INS: Companies which rely on the utilization of properties other than their own must be careful of the ramifications and associations that come along with these deals. There was a good deal of flap recently surrounding a major fast-food chain's promotion of the *Batman* movie via action figures, vehicles, etc., from the film. Some parents argued that the movie was too "dark" (suggesting evil) and too violent and they didn't like having the film's characters show up as toys/premiums at their local fast-food outlet.

Then there are aspects of quite controversial properties, such as *Beavis and Butt-head* and *South Park,* which, as part of their central approach to content, portray elements of the gross and disgusting side of humanity. While these shows may be appropriate for perhaps a 14-and-older target, their producers will likely agree that this type of content is not suited for a younger target. Any company that is targeting younger children would, of course, be well advised to be careful of associating itself or its products with properties that are not appropriate for their intended consumer/user.

PUBLICATIONS: Most publications, such as the majority of kid-targeted magazines (e.g., *Sports Illustrated for Kids, Disney Adventures,* and *National Geographic World*), portray individuals in positive and realistic ways. There are other publications such as comic books (mostly read by boys), which are often guilty of excessive violence, sexuality, and cultural and gender stereotyping.

RADIO: Radio programming targeted toward kids is relatively free from empowerment issues. Most radio programming is music, however, and we're all familiar with the controversy that surrounds certain dark, antisocial, excessively violent, sometimes sexist or too-sexual song lyrics. Radio executives would do well to screen more closely the kinds of messages they are sending over the airwaves, and parents would do well to monitor their children's music-listening carefully.

THE INTERNET: There has been much controversy of late regarding freedom of speech and the Internet. Especially given the accessibility of sexually explicit visuals and sexually oriented "chat" or interactions to any 8-year-old who can sufficiently navigate this newest of mediums, this is a real and present danger that calls for responsible intervention on the part of aware and caring adults.

In the above paragraphs we have raised a great many red flags of caution to product and program developers. We also issue these individuals a challenge. That challenge is to turn their efforts toward the creation and development of wholesome, empowering products and programs. A hundred years from now, just about all the adults who are presently alive will be gone, having passed the torch of civilization on to today's children and their children. Will that torch be used to burn down the greatest and finest of attitudes and institutions within us, or will it be used to set alight a world in which humanity rises above the ashes of its own darker tendencies and shines like a beacon of possibility and hope? It will be up to you and it will be up to me and the day-by-day decisions that we make on behalf of our children.

As you advance through the chapters of *What Kids Buy and Why,* ask yourself: These products and programs that I am developing and marketing—are these the types of products or programs that I would want my own child to have, watch, play with? If the answer is "Yes," then go for it with all you have. If not, then don't pursue it. It's as simple as that.

CHAPTER 3

THE YMS GUIDE TO SUCCESSFUL PRODUCT AND PROGRAM DEVELOPMENT

It is certain that success hinges on the ability to innovate. Nothing can replace the power of a solid new idea that contains within it a difference that makes a difference. But even the most original kid-targeted ideas can fail in the marketplace if not developed correctly—that is, with the needs, abilities, and interests of kids guiding the development at every turn. The YMS Product Leverage Matrix (Figure 3.1) was developed with just this need in mind—to help identify and then resolve all the critical issues that inevitably arise during the development and marketing process.

While there may be no Winning Formula that will guarantee success in developing new products or programs from scratch, the YMS approach will maximize your chances for success. In this chapter we outline a step-by-step plan to successful product and program development. As we proceed through each of the steps we will provide examples, and we will also build a product line from scratch as a further illustration of using the Matrix as a guide through the creative process. We'll refer to this innovative product line as Project X.

THE YMS PROCESS

STEP I: IDENTIFY YOUR MEDIUM

The first step is the easiest: identify what product or program medium you are working in. For example, if you are inside a learning-software company

FIGURE 3.1: THE PRODUCT LEVERAGE MATRIX

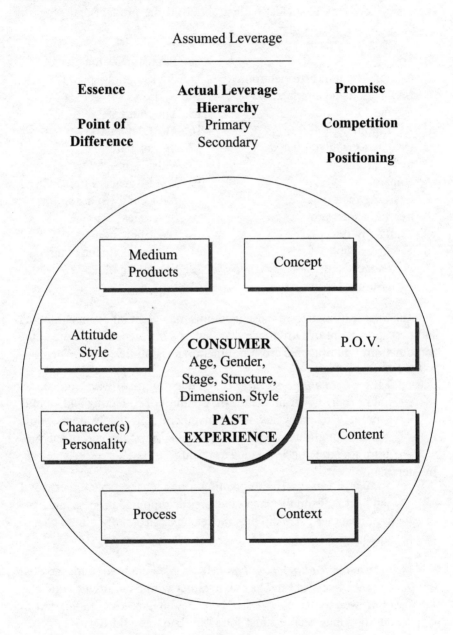

you are going to want to create innovative software, not new approaches to cheese-and-cracker snacks. However, the exercise of listing all related and even seemingly unrelated product and program mediums may produce surprising ideas. Here's a list of just about all the product and program mediums that relate to kids:

1. Toys
2. Games—board, card, electronic
3. Live-action and animated TV shows
4. Art supplies
5. Live-action and animated feature films
6. Apparel
7. Learning materials
8. Learning software
9. Craft activities
10. TV advertising
11. Print advertising
12. Promotions/Tie-ins
13. Publishing—magazines, books, newspapers
14. Radio
15. The Internet
16. The telephone
17. Sports items
18. Music tapes, CDs
19. Food—grocery items, fast food, candy, snacks, beverages
20. Electronic items
21. Personal hygiene items
22. School supplies

The cross-pollination of these mediums may yield innovative thinking and perhaps a Point of Difference that makes a difference. Here are some combinations that illustrate cross-pollination possibilities:

Toys + Learning Software: If I'm a learning-software company, I might "borrow" from the toy play pattern of collecting and include a process whereby my user/consumers collect key items while going through the program to be cashed in at the end of the program for strategic advantage or reward.

Snacks + Candy: If I'm creating a new cheese snack, perhaps I can borrow from the candy industry a "dipping" process and have my consumer/users dip the cracker snack in a multicolored cheese spread.

Internet + Radio + Fast Food: If I'm designing a youth-targeted Internet website, I might link together with a children's radio station, such as Radio AAHS or Disney or Fox kids' radio, and in addition may secure a fast-food "sponsor" as a third partner.

Electronic Items + Music + School Supplies: If I'm designing an innovative approach to a student's organizer notebook, I might allow for pockets that hold CDs and tapes, include a popular music CD in the organizer, and in addition, might "build in" a calculator and daily electronic organizer/calendar.

Example: Project X

Category: Manipulative preschool playsets, e.g., a playset barn or house or garage; a "manipulative playset" is typically made up of at least one building such as a barn and has play accessories such as farm animals, a tractor, and little farmer people.

Medium: Toys, preschool

Cross-pollination: *Electronics + learning software;* the innovation here is the possibility of incorporating electronic sounds, words, and/or phrases into the playset line. In addition, what about incorporating actual preschool-appropriate software into the playset?

STEP II: IDENTIFY TARGET CONSUMER(S)

Fundamental to the development of a winning product or program is the *accurate* identification of the target audience, and that's why the Consumer is central to the YMS Matrix. There are several key questions that need answers in order to be precise in this important step:

A. AGE RANGE: What is the age range of your target—3 through 8? 4 through 12? Are you crossing over age-segmentation lines that you need to take into account? With the product or program you are developing, can you cross these lines successfully or not? Can you make adjustments which will allow for cross-over or is your concept inherently limited in its appeal to a narrow age spread?

Important: An in-depth knowledge of the differences between individuals of different ages and developmental stages is critical to this determination. Chapters 4 through 8 detail each of the five developmental stages and provide all the information you should need in order to be accurate in age targeting. You may also want to read Chapter 9 on gender differences and Chapter 11 on kids and characters before returning to this chapter.

B. GENDER: What about gender differences? Is your product or program intended for both males and females equally? Or more for males or for females? (See Chapter 9.)

C. DEMOGRAPHICS/PSYCHOGRAPHICS: Are there any particular aspects of your target(s) that need to be taken into account such as regional differences, sociocultural differences, and even differing belief and values systems of different groups? For example, if your product is sports oriented, you may want to determine if there is a particular set of attitudes or behavioral predispositions to be considered, such as increased competitiveness or identification with particular athletic stars, particular sports, or particular teams.

In addition, do you know the answer to this important question: What are the predispositions and attitudes of your targeted consumer toward your medium and toward your type of product or program? For example, let's say you are intent on developing a nineties version of an electronic talking stuffed animal to follow on the heels of the success of Teddy Ruxpin of the 1980s. What are the predispositions of Moms these days regarding such an electronic toy? Why isn't Teddy Ruxpin still in the marketplace today? What do today's kids think of your idea? Have you tested it with them?

D. OTHER TARGETS: Do I have a dual target to contend with? For example, in the case of learning software I need to take into account the key *purchasers* (parents, often with Dad taking the lead) as well as the end user, the child. In the case of lunchbox-type snack foods I need to consider that I have two targets: Mom as the key purchaser and the child as the consumer.

Example: **Project X,** Manipulative Playset

Primary Target: Boys and girls equally, ages 2 through 5.

Secondary Target: Parents of 2-through-5-year-olds with primary emphasis on Moms as purchasers.

STEP III: KNOW YOUR COMPETITION

A variety of issues regarding your competition demand clear identification:

A. NUMBERS: Find out who the leaders are in your product/program category. What are the numbers, i.e., gross sales for each of their products or programs? What are the price points? The margins?

B. KEY FEATURES: From the consumer/user's point of view, what are the key features and benefits of each of your main competitor's products?

C. CONSUMER ATTITUDES: What are people saying about your competition? What do they like? What don't they like? What do they want that isn't being provided? What are they willing to pay for products of this type?

D. THE TRADE: What are trade attitudes toward your competition? What are buyers saying?

COMPETITION OF PROJECT X: Fisher-Price playsets, Playskool playsets, Mattel playsets, Tomy playsets, generic playsets.

> *Numbers:* Fisher-Price and Mattel are the leaders in the manipulative-playset medium with gross sales of $60 million annually. Price points range from $19.95 for smallest playsets to $89.95 for largest. Profit margins: 30 percent at wholesale. (This information is hypothetical; companies do not typically release such figures.)

> *Key Features:* Most playsets have standard features such as doors and windows that open and close, plastic or wooden human figures that have bases that fit into certain places on the playset, and/or accessories such as the Fisher-Price Schoolbus, which has places for the toy child figures to sit. Some playsets, such as garages, have elevators to take figures and cars up and down the playset from one level to another. Some playsets have simple electronic aspects, such as a "Mooo" sound when the cow's barn door is opened.

> *Consumer and Trade Attitudes:* Consumer and trade attitudes are positive and strong toward this category of toys. Manipulative playsets are staples in the industry and are constant sellers.

Now that you've done your "homework" in the first three steps, you're ready to begin the creative and development process in earnest. At this point the process becomes nonlinear. We often need to have things be linear. That is, for example, first the Concept needs to be created, then its Content, then a strong Positioning, then Packaging and Advertising, etc. A really effective creative process, however, is more often than not nonlinear. At YMS we utilize a nonlinear creative process that focuses on and is designed to get at where the power is (we refer to it as "leverage") or where it could be in the Product or Program Concept.

Maybe the strongest leverage is in a character or in the characters that are a part of the product. The cereal industry certainly takes advantage of "character power" when they put large character images on their cereal box fronts, e.g., Tony the Tiger or a later licensing rage, such as Jim Car-

rey's *Mask* character or the *Animaniacs*. Or, maybe the power is in an innovative process. When Sega first came out with Sonic the Hedgehog it was
the breakthrough approach to Sonic's speed and the speed of game play
that were key process innovations. Related YMS research and experience
has shown strong interest, especially on the part of boys, in speed—
whether it be related to wind-up cars or electronic games. Speed = power
and fun. While there were many other features that had leverage in the
Sonic the Hedgehog game program, such as innovative game screens and
game play, it was this main character's speed and the speed of game play
that brought the greatest power to this new product introduction. Cecil the
Chicken could have been the central character and the game would likely
have succeeded just as well based on the innovative processes that were
designed into the game. (And by the way, Sonic the Hedgehog is an
"essenced" name in that it is tied directly to his key innovative attribute,
speed. His name is also a catchy and effective name, and he is a superlative
animal type with an attractive and involving character depiction—all of
which have added real leverage to the overall concept.)

It's all about creating a difference that makes a difference. Hundreds
of new products enter the youth-targeted market every year and those that
really succeed have one or more points of difference that have real leverage to them. As has been stated, these winning products also ideally get the
job done when it comes to packaging, advertising, and the other important
aspects of product development around the "wheel" of the YMS Product
Leverage Matrix.

The following elements of the Matrix are, for organizational purposes,
presented in a linear fashion, but the Step-by-Step approach to them shifts
to an approach that considers them all at once, as a whole, or at least as
fully interrelated elements.

STEP IV: CONCEPT, CONTENT, POINT OF DIFFERENCE, ESSENCE, PROCESS, PROMISE, POSITIONING, NAMING, CHARACTERS, CONTEXT, POINT OF VIEW, AND ATTITUDE/STYLE

Step IV can be, by its very nature, a very long step because the way YMS
proceeds at this point is to use the Product Leverage Matrix wheel in a
dynamic, nonlinear fashion rather than in a linear way. Our recommendation is that while considering each of the elements around the Matrix
wheel separately, they also be considered simultaneously, or at least in a
dynamic flow of interrelationships. So while they are presented below in a
linear fashion, they should be considered all at once, interrelated, and in no

particular sequence. As we proceed through each of the Matrix elements, we will continue to refer to examples which illustrate them, as well as continue to build our preschool playset idea.

CONCEPT: What is the central idea of the product or program?

> *Example:* A story about a stuffed bear that comes to life in the secret world of a little boy (*Winnie the Pooh*).
>
> Project X: Aha! An exciting Concept could come from the Process variable of the Matrix.
>
> What if we design our playset such that the little plastic play people have bases on them in common geometric forms, e.g., a circle character, a square one, and others with other-shaped bases, e.g., triangle, rectangle, oval, and star? The child uses these characters in "key" style to affect different occurrences in and around the playset line. For example, the square-based character inserts in a square "keyhole" next to the barn playset door. When turned, it opens the door. The star-based character inserts into a star-shaped "keyhole" in the tractor seat and turns the wheels in steering-wheel style. These same characters cause other things to happen around the playset as well, each time being used as keys to insert into same-shaped "keyholes" to produce different effects.
>
> Now, that's a difference that appears to make a difference!
>
> This approach to an innovative playset inherently includes educational/learning aspects:
>
> a. introduction to geometric shapes
> b. the learning involved in being able to match the character-base shapes with the appropriate "keyholes"
> c. the learning and practice of cause–effect relationships. See *Process* section for additional play patterns connected to this Concept/Point of Difference.

CONTENT: What is the visual and verbal Content of the Product or Program?

> *Example:* A circus animal cookie package with colorful animal visuals and the Name, Positioning, and Product descriptions verbally appearing on package
>
> Project X: Our preschool playset line might include:

1. A barn   3. A house   5. A treehouse
2. A garage 4. A fire truck 6. A playground

Space doesn't allow for detailing out all of what would be seen and spelled out on each of these playsets: their configurations, colorations, attributes, and features. Suffice it to say for our purposes at this point that each playset would be colorful and would have at least ten "cause–effect" features.

POINT OF DIFFERENCE: What makes your product or program distinct from competing product, and/or an entirely innovative item in your product or program medium? It can't be just any difference. It needs to be a difference that makes a difference.

Example: Electric lights on shoes

If we were to just put rainbow-colored shoestrings on sneakers as our P.O.D. (Point of Difference), that wouldn't necessarily be a sufficiently impactful P.O.D. But to put electric lights that flash each time a 5-year-old takes a step, that's quite another difference—one that is significant and has a great deal of "payoff" for the targeted child—especially if it's the first innovation of its kind in its category. Being the first of a kind can add a great deal of power.

Project X: Already discussed, the "key" aspect of the characters and playset items is our difference that makes a difference.

ESSENCE: "Essence" further defines and delineates the Concept as well as pointing to its power.

Example: The essence of M&M's candies might be said to be: "Fun, multi-colorful bite-sized chocolates." Reducing a concept to its core power in words often assists the product or program in staying true to its core leverage. It also assists in keeping associated efforts such as packaging and advertising true to the "essence" and power of the product/program.

Project X: Our playset line could be "essenced" as follows:

A preschool playset line with its "people" having unique geometric-shaped bases that work as "keys" to produce effects such as opening doors on playset items.

PROCESS: "Process" refers to how the consumer/user interfaces with the product or program.

Examples: Hot Wheels cars are collected, organized, pushed around by hand, admired, used in conjunction with mini-car accessories such as play garages, car washes, etc. In Nintendo's Mario Brothers electronic games, the player scores points as he maneuvers his way through and around a variety of obstacles and screens until he reaches the end point of the game. One might also refer to a specific process within a game, such as the unique process of making a game character do flips to avoid his enemies.

Project X: Already covered: Unique key process. In addition, special electronic visual (lights) and sound effects might be incorporated to be turned on and off by key characters.

Note: This is an excellent example of how the utilization of the YMS Product Leverage Matrix serves to expand and deepen a concept. By focusing on Process at this point, we are able to entertain the innovative idea of adding electronic sound and light effects to the playset concept.

PROMISE: What benefits or payoffs does your product offer to the purchaser and consumer/user?

Examples: Star Wars, the movie, promises two hours of excitement including engaging characters, outstanding special effects, and an involving storyline. The Nestlé Quik Bunny promises additional fun relating with the character as the child drinks her chocolate milk drink.

Project X: Our playset line promises the usual benefits of other preschool playsets, i.e., manipulative play with structures such as houses and garages as kids open doors, turn cranks, make elevators go up and down, play with accompanying animals, etc. In addition, the unique Promises/benefits of our playset line are:

1. Added fun of unique cause/effects throughout the line
2. "Edutainment" aspects of key play, specifically the cause/effect play, the geometric-shapes learning, and the matching involved
3. Also, if electronic visual and/or sound effects are incorporated into the line, this will provide another set of promised benefits.

NAMING: "Naming" is dealt with as part of "Concept" on the Product Leverage Matrix. The creation of a powerful and "essenced" name for a product or program is critical to its success.

Examples: Some examples of powerful and effective names/concepts: Batman, Sega's *NBA Jam* basketball game; Myst, a highly successful adventure/mystery game; the Cabbage Patch Kids. This name, by the way, is particularly interesting because it combines a unique context—that of a cabbage patch—with the character dolls themselves, providing at the same time a whole "back story" (Content) for the dolls and where they came from. This is an excellent example of effective cross-pollination around the Product Leverage Matrix.

Project X: A very strongly essenced name for our playset line could be "KEY KIDS"—using the unique shape-based characters as our point around which we can name the product line.

POSITIONING: This refers to how your product is perceived in the mind of the consumer.

Example: Is it "The Strongest Man in the Universe!" as was He-Man's positioning? Is it the gum with "the Fruitiest Flavors"? The purchaser/consumer's mind is very much like a series of mail slots into which he puts incoming information. If your product is positioned powerfully it can occupy a mail slot of its own—being the only one or the best one or some other superlative. Positioning a product or program effectively is often a missed opportunity. Look at the mileage, for example, that M&M's has received over many years from their innovative "process" positioning of "Melts in your mouth, not in your hands!"

Project X: There are a variety of approaches that might be utilized for positioning our playset line. One approach might be:

KEY KIDS
Put 'em In and Turn On the Fun Learning!

CHARACTERS: Are you planning to utilize characters as part of your product Content? The effective and strategic use of cartoon characters or real-life heroes such as movie and TV stars and athletes *can* add a great deal of power to your kid-targeted proposition.

Example: General Mills' knew the power and impact of characters years ago when they began using Olympic heroes and other sports heroes on their Wheaties boxes. The use of characters is no automatic given, however. First of all, many cartoon-like characters begin to lose their appeal as children move into the 8-to-12 "Rule/Role" stage of development. Secondly, there are characters and then there are characters. Some characters are outdated. Some are of minimal popularity or niched popularity. Some characters appeal to both males and females and others primarily to males or only to females.

Project X: Our little shape-based people figures are "characters" of a sort. While they are somewhat generic in their human characteristics, we could explore making them distinct personality types, i.e., one stronger, one goofy-looking, one freckle-faced, one thin, etc. In order to really set them apart from competing characters we might also consider "essencing" them directly to the "key" concept, e.g., by giving them large ears that facilitate their use as keys, making it easy for a child to turn them in the playset "keyholes."

CONTEXT: Context refers to both the time period the concept exists inside of and its geographical settings.

Examples:

Time: The popular TV series *Dinosaurs* is set in modern times but with characters who are obviously from another era—a unique twist. *Star Wars* takes place in the future; most TV sitcoms are set in the present day.

Geographical Setting: Mattel a few years back came out with Malibu Barbie®, placing Barbie and her friends in a Malibu beach setting complete with all the contextual trimmings of the ocean, beach, swimsuits, lifeguards, etc.—a great success for Mattel as it combined all the fun associations of summertime at the beach with the Barbie® doll's beach fashion wear and fun activities with her pals.

Project X:
Time: Present day. *Locales:* Our playset theme takes place in the consumer's local community and neighborhood.

Words of caution: Take care not to overemphasize the past or future with very young children (under 5) as they are very present-time oriented. Select contexts that are associated with fun and excitement as much as possible—although this is not to be taken as an immutable rule, as witness the cabbage-patch locale.

At YMS we also look at Context to ascertain and take into account our product's competitive "set" or category. In other words, what is the "competitive context"? You might not want to launch a new line of fashion-doll toys if you knew that four other companies were going to attempt a similar launch. Or, perhaps, if you knew that the past three attempts—which were not too unlike your own—failed miserably.

P.O.V.: P.O.V. stands for "Point of View."

> *Example:* If we were talking about a TV sitcom such as *Roseanne* we could say it has a relatively liberal point of view, while *Mr. Rogers' Neighborhood* is highly conservative. Sometimes P.O.V. can refer to a central theme or message inherent in a product or program.

> *Project X:* The creation of a preschool playset line of toys is a conservative action with an inherently conservative P.O.V.

ATTITUDE/STYLE: This refers to the executional elements and qualities of our product and its packaging—for example, its graphic style might be abstract or free-form or frenetic.

> *Examples: Kool-Aid* paks have an upbeat, happy, colorful Attitude/Style. Some chewing gums are packaged in very straightforward and conservative colors and graphics, indicating a conservative Attitude/Style, while others are packaged in bright neon colors with wild graphic designs, indicating a progressive and modern Attitude/Style.

> *Project X:* Our playset line is essentially conservative and straightforward in that our buildings and vehicles are graphically representative of real houses, garages, fire trucks. We definitely want bright, eye-catching preschool colors and fun graphics on our packaging—designed in such a way that the key benefit of the key characters is demonstrated.

This completes the initial creative process of inventing and developing a product from scratch. For our Project X, the "Key Kids" line of preschool playsets, for example, we now have all its parameters and key ingredients in place, from Name and Positioning to its main Benefits and its Point of Difference. Now what there is to do is to further develop the line, reexamine each of the assumptions made in the first round of ideation, then "flesh out" the line as it proceeds through the development process. (The "Key Kids" playset line is, by the way, an actual innovation of YMS. If interested, please contact YMS directly.)

As soon as early prototypes and illustrated drawings are in place, the recommendation is to test the idea (a) for its own power and viability (in this case with kids and Moms) and (b) against competing playset lines put to similar mediums, e.g., drawings of them by the same artist.

STEP V: QUALITATIVE TESTING

At YMS we do not refer to our qualitative testing as focus groups. We call them Subject Tests, in order to distinguish them from traditional approaches. What's different about a Subject Test is essentially:

A. PRODUCT/PROGRAM PREANALYSIS: In traditional Focus Groups there is of course some thinking about what to test for and how to organize the testing for maximum response. In the YMS approach, however, a thorough analysis of the strengths and weaknesses of the project to be tested is conducted first, utilizing the Product Leverage Matrix, and a proprietary system for analysis that has been developed by YMS for this purpose, as a guide. The net result of this analysis phase is a series of hypotheses about how kids are going to react to the stimulus or stimuli placed in front of them. The testing, therefore, is highly focused and intentional in terms of the types of information and responses we are looking for.

Example: If we were to test a new fast-food premium program tied to the latest Disney release—let's take *Hercules* for example—we might hypothesize that:

1. The age range that will be attracted and involved with such a premium program will be: boys and girls ages 3 through 7 with a core cohort aged 4 to 5½.
2. Boys primarily will be attracted to Hercules as the heroic character and then their second and third choices will be the dark-side characters—the chief villain and his sidekick.
3. Girls primarily will be attracted to the female lead character, to Hercules, and to key "pet" animals in the character mix.
4. Regarding accessories, boys primarily will be attracted to any vehicles and weapons (such as bows and arrows) that are in the line, while girls will be attracted to clothing and buildings, e.g., hut-like houses, or stables if they are included in the lineup.
5. Regarding the special bag packaging for children's meals, boys and girls alike will prefer visuals that tell the story of the *Hercules* conflict, e.g., depicting Hercules pitted against the "bad guys," over other approaches to packaging.

There could be other hypotheses, depending on what the client would like tested, e.g., testing for color preferences, graphic-design preferences, and preferences regarding certain play patterns. The point is, YMS does its Analysis first to "predict" how kids (or Moms) are going to respond, then sets out in the tests themselves to either corroborate or disprove the hypotheses.

B. TESTING STRATEGIES AND PROCEDURES: Also quite distinct from traditional focus-group approaches is YMS's procedure during the testing. Let's assume a test of approximately 48 child subjects from ages 4 through 9. Typically we organize them into groups of six for 20-minute to 30-minute sessions.

> *Examples:* Group 1 (3:00 to 3:30): 3 boys age 4 and 3 boys age 5
> Group 2 (3:30 to 4:00): 3 girls age 4 and 3 girls age 5
> Group 3 (4:00 to 4:30): 3 boys age 6 and 3 boys age 7
> Group 4 (4:30 to 5:00): 3 girls age 6 and 3 girls age 7
> 5:00 to 5:30: Dinner break
> Group 5 (5:30 to 6:00): 3 boys age 6 and 3 boys age 7
> Group 6 (6:00 to 6:30): 3 girls age 6 and 3 girls age 7
> Group 7 (6:30 to 7:00): 3 boys age 8 and 3 boys age 9
> Group 8 (7:00 to 7:30): 3 girls age 8 and 3 girls age 9

We doubled up on the 6- and 7-year-olds because, in this hypothetical case, we predicted that the 6-through-7-year-olds would be the "core" target.

Moderators: At YMS we always moderate the tests ourselves personally since we are the ones who did the preliminary Analysis of the project. Should other expert moderators be utilized, however, they need to be coached in the hypothetical assumptions that came out of the Analysis phase, so they can test for reactions to these elements.

Stimuli: The proper preparation of and presentation of the stimuli to be tested is essential. The proper preparation and use of stimuli is an area in which many product developers make fundamental errors due to a lack of in-depth understanding of how kids at different ages and stages of development perceive and process information. There are certain rules of thumb to follow, based on what kids at different ages and stages of development can and cannot do.

1. *Stimuli should be age-appropriate:* This means that if we are testing 4- and 5-year-olds, we shouldn't include too many

stimuli, stimuli that are too complex, or stimuli that require abstract thinking. Stimuli that require comprehension of verbal and auditory information, for example, are often too abstract for a child of this young age.

2. *Dichotomous choices:* Also for younger children, issues should be presented with simple choices between two or at the most three elements, i.e., Which hat do you like best? Do you like the bear's hat in the No. 1 drawing, the No. 2 drawing, or the No. 3 drawing?

3. *Recording their responses:* At YMS we almost always have kids respond secretly—either by finger signals behind their backs (they put one, two, or three fingers behind their backs as a vote for stimulus 1, 2, or 3). Or we ask them to whisper their response in one of our ears so no one else can hear their vote.

4. *Probing:* After their choices are in place, the moderator can "probe" their choices, i.e., by asking "Why did two of you choose Number Two?" or "What about Number Three did you like? Point to the part that you like the most. Now point to the hat you like the least. What don't you like about that hat?" Older children can of course handle more abstract stimuli and more complex questions.

C. QUANTITATIVE TESTING: Fundamentally, YMS's approach to quantitative testing parallels our approach to qualitative testing in that it assumes the preliminary Analysis phase in order to isolate the key aspects of the project to then emphasize in the quantitative testing. Of course the two procedures are distinct in that a typical quantitative test involves more respondents (at least 100 and ideally 200 or more), a one-on-one rather than a group approach, and a shorter interaction with each respondent.

STEP VI: FURTHER PRODUCT DEVELOPMENT

There are of course a great many steps left in order to successfully develop and market a product or program from its ideation phase all the way through its successful performance in the marketplace and then its ongoing maintenance there. Product packaging needs to be developed and freshened once in the marketplace, advertising approaches must be created and developed, product-line extensions and spin-offs may need to be developed, and licensing programs may need to be pursued if you have a hot property. The focus in this chapter, however, has been on the early stages of product ideation and development through the initial testing phase.

In the next chapter we will begin our exploration of each of the five age segments dealt with in this book, starting with the birth-through-2-year-old. Even though most product and program developers and marketers do not often target children this young (and when they do, they are typically targeting the mothers of birth-through-2-year-olds), it is important that this age segment be understood, because what is experienced now lays the groundwork for future kid consumers.

CHAPTER 4

BIRTH THROUGH AGE 2
The Dependency/Exploratory Stage

> The toddler's world is . . . "a place of rocks, trees, grass,
> bugs, sun, moon, wind, clouds, rain, snow, and a million
> things; a world that runs on principles, where cause and
> effect balance, where 'fall down, go boom' means skinned
> knees, where fire burns and hot means 'don't touch.'"
>
> —Joseph Chilton Pearce,
> *The Magical Child*[1]

This most precious and tender stage of development encompasses the
years between birth and the third birthday. We refer to this stage of
development as the Dependency/Exploratory Stage because it is a time
during which the infant or toddler is very vulnerable and very dependent
upon caretaking adults and siblings. It is also a period of great learning,
exploration, and discovery, especially of the child's physical environment.
A child of this age is a true explorer, feasting his eyes on any new thing,
crawling and toddling after toys, plants, pets, expensive vases—anything
he can grab, and putting just about anything and everything he can grab
into his mouth.

There are many developmental tasks that this infant/toddler must
accomplish, and of these many tasks there are two that are fundamental.
The first is to gain a solid sense of emotional security, especially through
bonding with Mom and through experiencing the love of Dad, family, and
intimate friends. The second developmental task is to "map in" basic experiences, basic learnings about the physical world and language, so that
future learning can take place efficiently and at maximum potential. "Mapping in" refers to the basic structuring and development of neurons as a
particular learning takes place, e.g., an infant learning to hold her bottle by
herself. More about this later, when we deal with the infant/toddler's neurological and cognitive development.

WINNING PRODUCTS

As you know, children of this young age do not purchase items on their own. As they approach the age of 3, they begin to influence what their parents buy, perhaps by reaching out for colorful packaging on shelves or asking for Froot Loops or pleading, "Daddy, I want the bunny!" Essentially, however, this age is dominated by parent-purchase, primarily Mom's purchase for the child. The predominant motivations of the parents, therefore, must be carefully considered when developing products and programs for this age range.

The Winning Products and Programs for this age range, therefore, will be those which are developed with the particular developmental needs of the birth-through-2-year-old clearly in mind, and which most effectively match the parents' perceptions of what this age child needs.

There are not a lot of surprises here. Well known are the successes of Fisher-Price and Playskool, for example, in leading the way in the development of early-play-and-learning toys and activities, such as manipulative toys, activity centers for the crib, and little ride-on vehicles. Most of today's parents appear to be well aware of the role that early stimulation plays in their child's development, and children's room environments reflect this awareness with a plethora of crib and floor toys and activities, as well as licensed characters that surround the child on wallpaper and inhabit curtains, bedsheets, pillows, and towels.

Life itself, complete with cupboards full of pots and pans and backyards full of dirt and grass and water hoses and mud puddles, provides a great deal of this learning. At the same time, however, given the love and safety needs of this birth-through-2-year-old, and given his play and exploratory activities, there is a great deal of room for innovative products to contribute to this infant/toddler's early stimulation and development.

Parents have a particular interest in the safety of their infant/toddlers. Toys that are safe, as well as strollers, cribs, clothes, shoes, and food that are safe and healthy and nurturing for the child, are most likely to have a chance for success in the marketplace. Those companies that provide and promote the safest, healthiest products will most surely shine at the checkout counter.

WINNING PROGRAMS

Let's focus on feature films, TV programming, and software, with the upper end of the birth-through-2-year-old stage of development in mind.

Before approximately 1½ to 2 years of age, even though babies may be propped up in front of the TV in their infant seats, and while they may pay attention for a while to the sights and sounds, their attention spans and needs are such that TV programming or feature films or software that target this group are neither practical nor ideal. There are few exceptions. A notable exception, however, is the *Babyscapes* infant-stimulation video—a sort of video mobile—which utilizes moving red, black, and white shapes that move to classical music. There is reason to believe that children as young as 18 months will pay attention sufficiently—for short periods of time—to such TV stimulation, and furthermore that this type of technological stimulation may increase and expand brain growth and development. We must caution parents and other caretakers, however, against using any type of television programming as a "baby-sitter." What this age child most needs is lots of loving and stimulating caretaker–child interactions.

After approximately age 1½ to 2 the situation changes. By approximately the age of 2 a toddler's attention span has increased to the point where he can spend longer periods with film or programming, even some forms of simple software. Again a caution: by the age of 6 many children are watching as much as six hours of television a day—that's more than forty hours a week. There is reason to believe that so much TV contributes to a variety of potential problems such as overweight (child obesity is on the rise in the United States) and there is even the possibility that excessive TV watching may stunt the child's imagination. Being force-fed thousands of visual images every day, the child does not have to exercise his imaginative "muscles" as he does when reading or being read to or when engaging in fantasy play around the house or outdoors.

FILM AND TELEVISION PROGRAMMING

What is it about a feature animation film such as *Beauty and the Beast* and TV shows such as *Sesame Street, Barney & Friends,* or *Mickey Mouse* that holds the attention of children from age 2 up to almost 3 years of age? There are a variety of elements:

A. ANIMALS: All of the above-mentioned programs feature caricaturized or cartoonized animals—birds, dog-like Muppets, friendly dinosaurs, mice, and so forth. Children are fascinated by and attracted to animals of all kinds. In fact, some research has shown that as much as 80 percent of children's dream content is of animals up to the age of about 6.[2] It appears that through animal dreams children work on the resolution of a variety of issues and fears that they are dealing with in their young lives.

B. SAFE, NURTURING CHARACTERS: Given the safety and nurturance needs of this age child, characters like Big Bird and Barney are designed to be round and nurturing and safe. (Regarding roundness, research has proven that as early as 18 months of age, children identify crooked, jagged lines as "bad guys" or things that could hurt you, and round, curving lines as being "good guys" or safe.[3] It's no accident that most of the Disney characters, for example are quite rounded in their design. Mickey himself, for example, has a very round head; it's also larger in proportion to his body, like an infant's head. Mickey also has round ears, rounded arms and legs, and roundish feet/shoes.

Notably, Mickey and his pals also have no teeth; they just sport gums, except for Goofy, who has a couple of safe, rounded-off teeth. (Interestingly, the very fact that the Disney lineup of characters has apparently been designed to be perceived as very safe and nonthreatening limits their appeal, to an extent, to children below the age of about 7. As we shall see, as children mature they—boys more than girls—demand more "edge" and more potential threat from their characters. Compare Warner Brothers' Tasmanian Devil, who often bares a ferocious mouthful of teeth, for example, with the very round and safe Big Bird of *Sesame Street*. The above-7-year old is, more often than not, going to gravitate toward the emotional stimulation present in more edgy characters such as Tasmanian Devil, Garfield, Ren and Stimpy, the X-Men, and even Bugs Bunny with his cutting wit.

C. PACE AND FOCUS: Children under 3 do not respond well to extremely fast-paced programming with quickly-changing scenes, images, and visual content. Their brains are simply not yet wired for this kind of pace; the necessary circuitry is not yet in place. Older children and adults, in fact, find these types of such relatively slow-paced shows as *Barney & Friends* or *Sesame Street* very boring for the most part because *they* are "wired" for a quicker pace. Children aged 3 and under need a much slower pace so they can focus on the individual images and characters. The younger child, during his "safety" developmental stage, needs a softer, more nurturing, slower environment.

SOFTWARE PROGRAMMING

Although computer programming is now being developed with the upper end of this birth-through-2-year age range in mind as a target, sitting at a keyboard in front of a computer screen—at least for any length of time—is not a good match with the developmental needs and abilities and attention span of this age range. This is a period of free play, of exploration of the physical environment, of right-brain developmental emphasis; this is not a time to be involved with essentially left-brained tasks at a computer.

At best it could be argued that very simple and fun edutainment programming, such as is employed in Sega's *Pico* Learning System, might be appropriate and involving for a segment of precocious almost-3 and 3+ year-olds. (*Pico* requires children to use a sort of electronic "pen" to point to objects on a book-like screen, and when they touch an object some "cause–effect" phenomenon occurs. For example, they might touch a picture of a car and the system responds with "This is a car: beep-beep!"). However, even with "appropriate" and age-graded hardware and software, caution should be employed so that a child of this age does not remain at overly structured activities such as this for very long. This age child needs to be the active little explorer that he is by nature, free to roam and experience at first hand without excessive structure.

The following list sets forth the core aspects of the development of the birth-through-2-year-old child.

Core Developmental Aspects

Needs/Wants	Physiological needs
	Love
	Sensory stimulation
	Safety
Cognition	Sensorimotor
Neurology	R System—Brain stem (0–7)
	M System—Limbic (1–11)
Perception	Reflexive
	Object constancy
	Object separation
Moral sense	Premoral
Self/Social	Symbiotic/Dependent
	Impulsive
Humor	Safe
	Surprise
	Simple slapstick
	High sensorimotor

Let's look briefly at each of the aspects listed above as well as any implications for product or program development that they might lead us to.

NEEDS AND WANTS

Most of what a child up to the age of approximately 3 needs has been pointed to already in this chapter—namely a secure, safe, loving environment in which a child can emotionally "bond" with his mother primarily, and secondarily with his father, other significant caretakers, and intimate family and friends. He also needs a great deal of stimulation, and we have touched on the stimuli of physical objects such as those found naturally in and around his home. We have not, however, talked about language development.

One of the key ways that the birth-through-2-year-old learns (in fact as early as the prenatal months) is through listening to the speech of the important people in his home—especially his mother and father. With each word, with each phrase, neural impact occurs, learning occurs. A child this age who grows up in an environment rich with language, especially language that is couched in soothing and nurturing tones, is busy developing the neuronal structures that facilitate language acquisition and facility. Conversely, children of this age who are raised in an environment that is limited in the language spoken to them—both in quality of language and quantity—will develop less language ability.

IMPLICATIONS

The implications for manufacturers and for Moms and Dads as purchasers are clear. Products and programs that provide a safe, stimulating, and emotionally nurturing environment are those that most contribute to the maximum development of the birth-through-2-year-old. Car seats and cribs and strollers that are ultrasafe, foods and beverages that are most nutritional, stuffed animals and warm blankies and toys that are comforting, engaging, and stimulating—these are the fare parents are most drawn to. While there may be little surprises here, there is a demand in this market for excellence and innovation and design beyond where we've gone before.

There are, however, many opportunities if we look in developmental corners where we haven't looked to any great extent before. Let's take the aforementioned arena of language development, for example. While nothing can replace hours and hours of Mom and Dad speaking in nurturing tones to the child, while nothing can replace lots of time spent reading to the child, where are the products and programs that could help Mom and Dad be yet more effective? Is there an early language-learning program that guides parents and spells out for them just which words and phrases are ideal for their child to have mastered at each stage of development?

In the late 1980s, Teddy Ruxpin appeared on the toy scene from Worlds of Wonder. Teddy was a stuffed bear whose mouth and eyes moved animatronically and in sync with specially programmed TV shows. Given the typical computer with its "cold personality" and highly structured technology, a direction for us to pursue, perhaps, is more software and hardware put into soft and accessible forms such as Teddy Ruxpin but designed for an even younger audience. Barney, a purple stuffed dinosaur, has recently appeared on the scene with some of these interactive capabilities. The authors applaud these efforts to facilitate fun language acquisition.

COGNITION AND NEUROLOGY

EARLY LEARNING

The child at birth primarily performs reflex actions. But by the second month of life the child is already differentiating among objects in the environment through his senses and through the sucking reflex. Between the fourth month and the eighth month, touch and vision begin to synchronize and coordinate. The child will now begin to grasp everything within visual range, indicating sensorimotor integration.

It is toward the end of the first year of life that a critical dimension of cognitive development takes place. The child begins to develop object permanence, in which objects outside the child take on a relatively permanent or fixed conceptual representation. Emerging now is the beginning of object size and shape constancy. Also in this 8-through-12-month-old phase, the child for the first time shows awareness of causality—awareness that objects (besides himself) can *cause* effects.

Early in the second year of life, truly intelligent behavior emerges. The child evolves new means of solving problems through experimentation. By the end of the second year, the child is developmentally ready to internally represent objects (symbol system development). This will liberate the child from pure sensorimotor intelligence and permit the intervention of new problem-solving processes—especially through language.

NEUROLOGICAL TASKS

Estimates of how many brain cells or "neurons" are present in the average brain range from billions to trillions, but what's important to know is what these neurons are "up to" at different ages and stages of development. In this chapter, and in each of the chapters on different ages and stages of child development that follow, we'll describe the central learning or "structuring" activity of the brain cells.

Young humans are essentially like learning machines. This learning begins before birth, but for purposes of simplicity and focus we'll begin with the infant/toddler stage of birth through his third year of life. This young brain/mind/body has so much to learn, and this early learning has been shown by Greenfield[4] to consist of three phases:

A. ROUGHING IN: As the child encounters a new stimulus, such as his mother's face, the first thing that occurs is that certain neurons establish themselves in a sort of neural "structure" to hold and remember that stimulus—a sort of rough sketch.

B. FILLING IN THE DETAILS: Each time the birth-through-2-year-old encounters the same or a similar stimulus, whether it's his mother's face, a stuffed giraffe, or a bird, the original "sketch" gets filled in with more and more details.

C. PRACTICE AND VARIATION: More and finer ability to distinguish among objects develops with practice, and important variations are recognized and established, such as moving from the concept *bird* to different kinds of birds, or from the task of opening a drawer to opening doors, cabinets, and suitcases.

The central learning/brain-development task of the birth-through-2-year-old, therefore, is to "map in" basic learnings about the physical environment and key people in his life. Have you ever watched a 1½-year-old play with a pile of sticks in the yard, in total concentration moving them this way and that, picking them up and putting them down? Have you ever observed as this age child toddles up to a kitchen cabinet and opens it and closes it and opens it and closes it and opens and closes it—sometimes to the annoyance or exasperation of his parents? What is this child up to? He is focused intently on the task of opening and closing: first roughing in the concept and the neuromuscular patterns, then filling in details and practicing to gain basic mastery over this activity. Later he will practice variations of opening and closing as well, perhaps with snaps or buttons or books.

He is so focused, in fact, that he often cannot even hear or otherwise pay attention to any other stimuli such as Mom telling him, "Billy, stop banging those doors open and closed!" In fact, if the child is continuously taken away from such "structuring in" activities, if he is interrupted, it is likely to interfere with his natural learning process; the "mapping in" of those neurological fields that are designed to be responsible for that type of activity gets interrupted.

EMOTIONAL SECURITY

There are many other learnings that this age child is involved in, the most important of which, according to many researchers such as Damasio,[5] Goleman,[6] and LeDoux,[7] is the emotional security and bonding that take place on various levels. More important perhaps, or certainly every bit as important as beginning mastery over his physical environment, this is the child's most critical stage for achieving emotional security—for feeling safe, feeling loved, feeling connected to the most important others in his life: his mother first and foremost, followed ideally by his father, then other family members, caretakers, and intimate family friends.

THE SEVEN INTELLIGENCES

In this first of five chapters dedicated to an in-depth understanding of each of the different age segments, it is important to stress the latest points of view regarding how many different arenas of learning exist. As product and program developers, marketers, and advertisers, it is critical to be aware of these different types of learnings as children grow through different ages and stages of development. Research headed by Howard Gardner of Harvard suggests that there are seven distinct "intelligences."[8] The number of intelligences present in human beings and the rationale by which something can be proven to be an intelligence are hotly debated issues. Although it is beyond the scope of this book to delve deeply into these matters, suffice it to say that Gardner and others are opening up new thinking that challenges restrictive, limited views of intelligence.

Figure 4.1 (p. 52) summarizes each of Gardner's seven intelligences.

WINDOWS OF OPPORTUNITY

While all seven intelligences are being developed or otherwise impacted in some degree throughout a person's life, there are critical periods, or "windows of opportunity," during which the development of particular intelligences/skills is most focused. Many of the most essential and foundational learnings, in fact, occur before the age of approximately 11. Importantly, it has been suggested by Joseph Chilton Pearce that at approximately the age of 10 or 11 there is a major "cleanse" that occurs within the brain, in which all unmyelinated neurons (those neurons and neuronal structures that have not been protected by myelinating sheaths) are "swept out"—ideally leaving a much more efficient brain behind.[9]

The problem with this is that if key neuronal structures having to do with different kinds of learnings and learning capacities and abilities (such as first and second language learning or emotional awareness and expression) have not been firmly established by this time, then this "foundational" period is over and the window of opportunity closed—leaving the individual "handicapped" or at least not fully developed in one or more

FIGURE 4.1: GARDNER'S SEVEN INTELLIGENCES

Logical/Mathematical Intelligence

Often called "scientific thinking," this intelligence deals with inductive and deductive thinking/reasoning, numbers and the recognition of abstract patterns.

Visual/Spatial Intelligence

This intelligence, which relies on the sense of sight and being able to visualize an object, includes the ability to create internal mental images/pictures.

Body/Kinesthetic Intelligence

This intelligence is related to physical movement and the knowings/wisdom of the body, including the brain's motor cortex, which controls bodily motion.

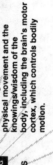

7

WAYS OF KNOWING

MULTIPLE INTELLIGENCES

Musical/Rhythmic Intelligence

This intelligence is based on the recognition of tonal patterns, including various environmental sounds, and on a sensitivity to rhythm and beats.

Verbal/Linguistic Intelligence

This intelligence, which is related to words and language—written and spoken—dominates most Western educational systems.

Intrapersonal Intelligence

This intelligence relates to inner states of being, self-reflection, metacognition (i.e. thinking about thinking) and awareness of spiritual realities.

Interpersonal Intelligence

This intelligence operates primarily through person-to-person relationships and communication.

Source: David Lazear, *Seven Ways of Knowing: Teaching for Multiple Intelligences* © 1991 by IRI Skylight Training and Publishing, Inc., Arlington Heights, Ill. Reprinted with permission.

areas. Furthermore, since the "window of opportunity" for maximum neuronal "structuring in" of certain capabilities is closed, the opportunity for maximum learning of these capabilities is also closed, making learning of these particular capabilities more difficult. Figure 4.2 shows these "critical periods" from prenatal months to the age of 10.

FIGURE 4.2: CRITICAL PERIODS

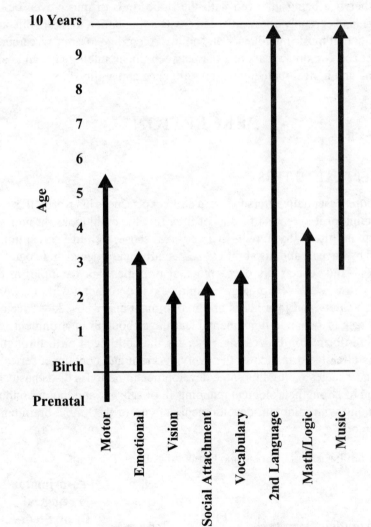

IMPLICATIONS

As can be easily discerned from Figure 4.2, the period from the prenatal months up to the age of 3 is perhaps the most critical period of all for learning. The child's need for love and emotional safety is especially intense at this time. Foundational learnings are also occurring in motor skills, early language, and mathematics.

Regarding music, although the critical period for music acquisition may not begin until approximately age 2½, indications are that listening to and otherwise being involved with the right kinds of music even before this age, and certainly afterwards, can create a foundation for more effective acquisition of music intelligence and ability. According to some researchers, a direct correlation appears to exist between music intelligence and early learning and logical/mathematical intelligence and ability.[10]

PERCEPTION

PERCEPTUAL FILTERS

Perception essentially refers to how a child experiences his world. It is useful to think of it in terms of a sort of filter that the child looks through—a "perceptual filter," if you will. In a very real sense, a child's perception is shaped by his past and his abilities—especially neurological and cognitive abilities—and reflects his developmental priorities. For example, in the model below, we have a prelogical child who is perceiving within a world in which safety and love needs are predominant and whose key developmental task is to map in fundamental learnings about his environment.

The Information Processing Filter for the child aged birth through 2 years is directly correlated to the evolving brain and contains a series of subsidiary stages within this same developmental period. This is basically a period of strong neurological mapping-in of sensory and motor connections along with midbrain-development activity of the limbic brain emotion centers.

FIGURE 4.3: INFORMATION PROCESSING FILTER: AGES BIRTH THROUGH 2

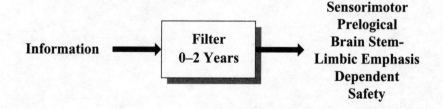

At this young stage of development the cognitive aspects of brain activities are very simple and concrete with the integration of object permanence, size and shape constancy, and simple and concrete cause–effect connections. The child in this developmental period is basically prelogical, with the beginnings of symbolic translation by the end of the second year of life. This is also a period of great dependency and need for safety. The parent or parental substitute plays a critical role as the child's touchstone for emotional stability and support.

There are several critical developments with regard to information-processing at this earliest stage of development:

A. OBJECT CONCEPT: The term *object concept* refers to the idea that objects in the environment (visual cues) must be coded by the child at this developmental stage through the integration of sensori-motor skills and early cognition so that these objects can be conceptualized as separate from himself. At birth the infant has no such understanding or awareness of objects as such, no sense of self, and essentially cannot differentiate himself from the objects and individuals around him. As development unfolds, the child gains this understanding of objects as separate from himself primarily through the integration of sensory and motor activities and the increased cognitive abilities that accompany his growing understanding.

B. CAUSALITY: The term *causality* refers to the child's ability to understand the relationship between cause and effect. At birth the child has no understanding of causality, yet intuitively and reactively can "cause" Mommy to come to his aid when hungry or in stress. This ability to understand that he himself causes things to happen, e.g., a mobile to move, evolves as early as age four months and continues in sophistication and complexity through the first three years of life and of course beyond.

C. INTENTIONALITY OR GOAL-DIRECTED BEHAVIORS: Deliberate behaviors emerge approximately four months after birth, when the child's behaviors become increasingly oriented toward objects and events outside the body. The young child tries to repeat or reproduce events that have occurred. Play elements attached to a crib that allow for repetitive sensorimotor behaviors are a natural part of this developmental unfolding. As the child moves toward internal representations of these objects, the need for greater levels of complexity increases.

THE MORAL SENSE

The first three years of life are essentially "premoral" in that the cognitive abilities have not yet matured sufficiently to allow the child to make judgments regarding good-bad, right-wrong. During the "terrible twos" the child is learning "No" rapidly and sometimes to the chagrin of frustrated parents, but this is more of a stimulus–response-based kind of learning than one which involves any sophisticated form of judgment.

SELF/SOCIAL DEVELOPMENT

Socially, this is a stage of dependency—especially on one's parents and primary caretakers—and self-centered impulsivity. While the beginnings of independence are present in the third year of life (the "terrible twos") this toddler is still symbiotically dependent upon her immediate caretakers. She is naturally self-centered and impulsive. The world really *does* revolve around her every want and need, and she has, overall, very little real sense of what another might need or be feeling. (Interestingly, research shows that female infants tend to be more sensitive to the upsets of other babies in their environment than male infants are.)

This child may participate with such others as family members or other children in some play activity, but there is very little real cooperative or interactive play. In the midst of playing house, for example, the 2-year-old is not likely to conform to his older sibling's wishes that he stay put and pretend to be the family dog; instead he'll be distracted by the first thing that comes along and go off on his own to pursue It.

IMPLICATIONS

There are two important implications that can be drawn from the birth-through-2-year-old's limited social development and impulsivity.

A. PARALLEL PLAY: Manufacturers and parents alike will be well advised not to design play activities for the birth-through-2-year-old that ask him to cooperatively play or otherwise meaningfully interact with others. Instead, expect this age child to "parallel play," that is, to be engaged in "his own thing" alongside others.

B. ATTENTION SPAN: Most people think that the attention span of the birth-through-2-year-old is very short-lived. While this may be true of activities that are structured or otherwise set up for the child, it is not true of activities that he is genuinely and intensely engaged in.

As explained before, once the child finds a new activity to be "mapped in," such as opening and closing, or the discovery of all the aspects of a new puppy experienced for the first time, the child's attention span and focus can be intense and prolonged. The indication for manufacturers and parents here is to come up with basic learning activities that will engage the child in a sustained way.

HUMOR

Since much humor is based on language that this age child does not yet have in place, humor for the birth-through-2-year-old is of the most basic variety. It primarily consists of smiling and laughing and tussling and wrestling about with his parents, siblings, other relatives, and intimate friends.

In addition there is the well-known peek-a-boo phenomenon at this age. Everyone has seen how extremely tickled—sometimes to the point of hysterical giggling—a 1-year-old can get playing peek-a-boo, but not everyone understands quite why peek-a-boo is so humorous. It's actually related to a cognitive ability that has yet to develop and is related directly to "object constancy."[11] The young child's neurology and cognitive development have not yet allowed him to understand that when an object (or Mommy's face) disappears behind a towel, it is still there. It is literally "out of sight and out of mind." So when it reappears again it is unexpected; it's as if it reappears from nowhere and it surprises and startles the child humorously.

IMPLICATIONS

Given the selective attention spans and limited humor styles that engage the birth-through-2-year-old, the implications for approaches to humor are twofold.

A. MAKE IT FUN: Manufacturers and parents alike should design fun play objects and interactions that facilitate physical fun, i.e., lots of holding and touching, lots of love/play interaction between the child and his intimates.

B. KEEP IT SIMPLE: Approaches to too-sophisticated humor (that is, TV or software content that is fundamentally linear and logical in its approach) will be over the heads of children in their first three years of life.

SUMMARY

By way of summarizing the foregoing information on the birth through 2-year-old, let's revisit the YMS Product Leverage Matrix, now Figure 4.4, and highlight the most important elements of the Matrix as they apply to key categories of products and programs.

CONCEPT AND CONTENT: Any product or program Concepts, and their Content, designed for the birth-through-2-year-old will of necessity need to be of the simplest nature. Whether it is a simple manipulative stacking toy or a pair of toddler sneakers, too much complexity can cause problems.

POINT OF VIEW (P.O.V.) AND ATTITUDE/STYLE: *Point of View (P.O.V.)* refers to the underlying philosophy or messages that accompany a product or program. For example, is it conservative or liberal? Safe and nurturing or controversial and edgy? For this young and vulnerable child, a product or program's Point of View, its "Attitude," and its approaches to marketing and advertising, need to be safe, stimulating, conservative, non-edgy, and loving.

CONTEXT: *Context* refers to the geographical or physical setting of a product or program, and to its time period. For this age child, settings need to be localized around home and family, and any approaches to time must be present-day oriented and not related to the past or future; this age child simply does not yet have the cognitive capacity to understand or relate to times other than the present.

CHARACTERS: The kinds of characters that the birth-through-2-year-old is most likely to gravitate toward and become involved with are characters such as the Disney characters, Barney, Big Bird and the *Sesame Street* gang, and other rounded, safe, nonthreatening, non-edgy characters. Softer versions of the Warner Brothers cartoon-character lineup, such as the *Tiny Toons* characters, are also very appropriate. Children especially of this age and even older, up to approximately 5, are very visual in their orientation to the world and certainly to characters. In other words, what they will be paying attention to is not the content of what characters are up to, nor is it what characters are saying; instead, they are mostly entertained by their cute, funny, colorful faces and bodies, and by the animated action itself, along with the accompanying music and sound effects.

FIGURE 4.4: THE PRODUCT LEVERAGE MATRIX

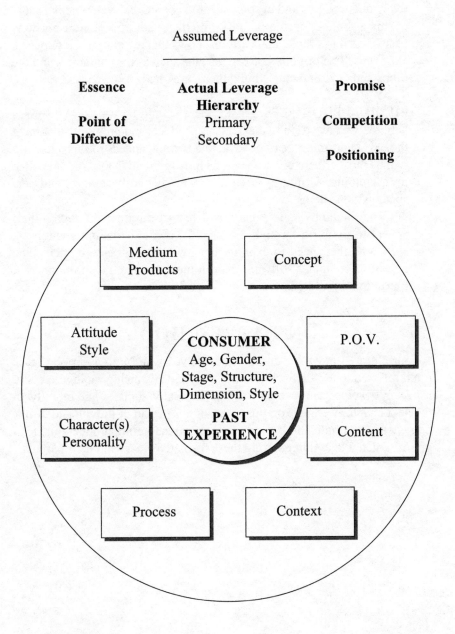

PROCESS: *Process* refers to such things as pacing, music, sounds and sound effects, and to the interactive process of how a child is to interact with a toy or book, audiotape or cartoon show. Due to the relatively undeveloped and unsophisticated cognitive developmental stage of this age child, pacing is most effective when it is slower, music is best when it is simple, and cartoon shows that are simple, slow-paced, and focused on brightly colored visuals, such as the characters and the props and environments around them, are ideal.

MEDIUM/PRODUCTS: Again, there should be very few surprises here. As we have tried to make clear, products and programs that meet the basic nurturance, safety, love, and stimulus needs of this age child will be most effective. These will be mostly found in the "mediums" of toys, clothing, furniture, room decor, foods and beverages, and personal hygiene items.

The mediums of television and feature film are limited in their appeal to the birth-through-2-year-olds, given their limited attention spans and their need to explore their real physical environment. The appeal of computer software is even more limited, given its inherent linear, too-structured process.

ON TO PRESCHOOL

As our children move beyond the toddler years and into a period that is often referred to as "early childhood," they are advancing rapidly in every aspect of development—cognitively, perceptually, socially, and morally. In the next chapter we focus on this 3-through-7 period of growth and development and its implications for designing and marketing products and programs targeted to children during these formative years and their parents.

CHAPTER 5

AGES 3 THROUGH 7
The Emerging-Autonomy Stage

Children are natural mythologists: they beg to be told
tales, and love not only to invent but to enact falsehoods.
—George Santayana,
Dialogues in Limbo[1]

This is a most magical stage of childhood. It is this early childhood
period that is the most filled with what we grown-ups think of as
childish: play, fantasy, surprise, pretend—a time when the imagination
reigns supreme and anything is possible.

The ages of 3 through 7 are a time for playing house and building forts
out of couch cushions, a time for cops and robbers, a time for dress-up and
Hi-Ho! Cherry-O games, a time to begin diving into Mario Brothers and
computer games, a time for Mickey Mouse and *Animaniacs* and the *Power
Rangers* show and—yes—still a time for Santa Claus.

Child psychologists have long promoted the fact that children learn
critical lessons through their play, and this 3-through-7 period is filled with
hours and hours spent at play. For the product and program developer, play
isn't all there is to be focused on because, after all, 3-through-7-year-olds
still need clothes and shoes (the latest hot tennies), cereal, learning software, and vitamins. But in terms of what most product, program, and marketing efforts are trying to accomplish, *fun* and *play* are the bywords and
the essence of what the 3-through-7-year-old is about.

We must make clear that each of the age ranges presented in this
book—in this case 3-to-7-year-olds—represents a wide gamut filled with a
great many changes in abilities, behaviors, perceptions, etc. A 3-year-old
is very different from a 7-year-old in many ways. A common denominator,
however, is the key reason why these ages are grouped or "segmented" in
this way: 3-through-7-year-olds (approximately) share a relatively stable
stage of brain development regarding emotion and cognition.[2] One cannot

be overly simplistic about these "age segments," however. While it is true that during this 3-through-7 period the central thrust of brain development affects areas of the brain which facilitate the imagination, other parts of the brain are developing as well—readying the child for the next stage of his development.

WINNERS

There are of course a great many products and programs that could be named as winning or successful for this 3-through-7 age range. As we attempt to get at what "wins" with the 3-through-7-year-old, let's focus on two of them that have been megahits: the Cabbage Patch Kids and the Power Rangers.

THE CABBAGE PATCH KIDS PHENOMENON

Beyond the fact that the Cabbage Patch Kids dolls effectively provide a child with basic doll play, there are several key reasons why the Cabbage Patch Kids dolls were so successful in the 1980s and why they have retained a certain popularity into the 1990s. In order of their importance, these reasons are set out below.

> **A. IDENTIFICATION:** A core principle that underlies the importance of and success of dolls and doll play is Identification or Identification Patterns. An Identification Pattern is essentially the *relationship or association* that the child has with a toy that is human or animal in nature—that is, how a child relates to and interacts with the human or animal toy object. YMS has discovered that there are essentially four Identification Patterns that children experience in their relationships to dolls, animals, and characters of all types:
>
>> *1. Nurturing:* In this relationship, the child either nurtures the toy doll, animal, or character (e.g., a Cabbage Patch Kid or a generic baby doll), or she is nurtured by it (e.g., Big Bird, Mr. Rogers, Barney).
>>
>> *2. Like Me:* A "Like Me" relationship or identification pattern with a doll or other object means that the child relates to the doll, animal, etc., as like himself or herself. For example, a little girl might see a Strawberry Shortcake minidoll or a Polly Pockets minidoll as somewhat like herself—as a little girl of approximately her own age. A child may also see certain qualities in a

character that are similar to qualities he or she sees in the self and perceives them to be "like me." A child may identify with Garfield's indolence, for example, or with his gluttony.

3. *Emulatory:* In an "Emulatory" Identification Pattern, the child emulates or wants to be like the human or animal or character (e.g., a Batman figure, a Barbie® doll) and/or wants to possess certain of their characteristics or ways of being.

4. *Disidentification:* This is a different type of Identification, in which the child does *not* want to be like a human or animal character but is attracted to and involved with it because of its "dark side," or negative attributes. (Villains are typical objects of disidentification, e.g., Darth Vader of *Star Wars,* Skeletor of He-Man fame, or "soft" villains such as Wile E. Coyote in *Road Runner,* or Gargamel of the Smurfs.

The first form of Identification—Nurturing Identification—is, in our view, the fundamental reason why the Cabbage Patch Kids dolls have been so successful. Other dolls, especially baby dolls, are also based on this type of nurturing identification, but the Cabbage Patch Kids dolls have taken providing nurturance to new emotional depths with their adoption premise.

Because of their adoption positioning, these baby dolls were "crying out" to be adopted. This adoption aspect set up a greater "this baby doll needs me" response on the part of the child than could have been achieved without this adoption approach. Although it may appear on the surface to be ludicrous, the subconscious response on the part of children (especially girls who appear to have more nurturing instincts than boys) might be something like: "What, not adopt them and allow them to be poor orphaned waifs? No, this doll needs a home and needs me!"

B. PHYSICAL EXECUTION: There were also physical aspects of these Cabbage Patch Kids dolls that worked together with and enhanced this "they need me" emotional response:

1. *Their physical appearance*—especially their broad, dimpled faces and hands and feet—communicated babyish qualities that invited nurturance.

2. *Their pose*—with arms outstretched—appeared to say: "Please pick me up, I need you!"

The "look" or physical appearance of the Cabbage Patch Kids dolls has been the subject of much controversy. Some adults in particular questioned: "How can these ugly or at best odd-looking dolls be so popular?" Many of them explained it away as being a complete marketing ploy based on the adoption angle or the fact that there was a scarcity of Cabbage Patch Kids dolls at the peak of their early success.

While it is true that the adoption premise was central to the success of the dolls, and it is also true that their popularity and the demand for them created a scarcity that generated a great deal of publicity and increased demand, an important point needs to be made here regarding the differences between adult and child perception. The typical adult "sees" or perceives a Cabbage Patch Kid doll's face quite differently from the way a 3-through-7-year-old sees it.

Through the analytical, logical "filter" of perception of many adults a Cabbage Patch Kid doll face may appear to be weird or unnatural, even unattractive or ugly. But from the perceptual filter that children look through, this is not likely to be the case; they are more likely to see in a Cabbage Patch Kid's face features of a baby that are exaggerated and therefore quite appealing: round, broad faces with large dimples and a baldish forehead.

Differences in perception between adults and children should not be underestimated in terms of their importance for anyone interested in developing or marketing products and programs to children (and to their parents). Adult developers and marketers should take great care to examine their assumptions about what they believe will appeal to children at different ages and stages of development. Adults and children are not looking at the world through the same windows.

C. PERSONALIZATION: The fact that each Cabbage Patch Kid doll had his/her own special name, making no two alike, makes the child feel very strongly, "This doll is mine, is special, and no other is like it." This "personalization" was another angle present in this megahit phenomenon that increased the "payoff" inherent in having a Cabbage Patch Kid doll. This is related to "Identification" in that it also cemented and made more real the relationship or bond between the child and the doll. The 3-through-7-year-old stage of development is very much an egocentric period; a greater sense of "mine" due to the personalization of these dolls lends them a greater appeal. This is an excellent example of how—in this case with its personalization angle—a product can "match up" closely with a developmental stage of children.

Importantly, from a business point of view, this naming/personalization angle, along with their customized dress and slightly different "looks," also greatly enhanced children's desire to have more than one doll and even to become a collector of the dolls.

D. POINT OF DIFFERENCE: In any product or program arena, it is vital to present something that is unique, that has an attractive and involving Point of Difference or Points of Difference from competing concepts that have gone before or are currently in the marketplace. The human mind is much like a computer in the sense that it quickly categorizes new stimuli as "like" or "the same as" other known stimuli. Human beings crave the new and different—and children are no exception. They are always wanting ("But, Mom, I've got to have it!") whatever is new—be it the latest and most popular electronic game or action figure, or permutation of the Barbie® doll.

The unique "look" of the Cabbage Patch Kids dolls coupled with the uniqueness of the adoption premise succeeded very well in setting them apart with a Point of Difference that made a difference in the marketplace. It needs to be stressed again and again that it's not enough to merely have a Point of Difference. A Point of Difference must be impactful enough to separate itself from the competition in a meaningful way in order to really make a difference—*a difference that really makes a difference.*

Nurturing Identification, Personalization, and Point of Difference, from the YMS perspective, are the three core reasons that carried Cabbage Patch Kids dolls to megahit status. One might say that the "designer" aspect of the dolls—they were signed by their designer, Xavier Roberts—had some positive effect on parents as well. The excellence of their execution—the attention to detail and the quality in their dress and design—also played a role. And certainly it could be added that these dolls delivered solid traditional doll play: holding, pretend feeding, changing diapers and clothes, and accessory play such as with special Cabbage Patch Kids doll accessories. But these were not the aspects of this product line that made the difference in the marketplace. It was the *emotional response* that these unique dolls elicited—due to the adoption and personalization angles along with their innocent and needy physical appearances and poses—that lifted them to the top.

POWER RANGERS: MEGAHIT OF THE NINETIES

As with the Cabbage Patch Kids dolls, many are the adults who have wondered what it is about the Power Rangers that creates such a strong reaction on the part of children, especially children in this 3-through-7 age range. For those who may not be familiar with the Power Rangers, they are a team of three young men and two young women (in their late teens to early twenties) who *transform* from relatively ordinary urban youth into a team of uniformed Rangers who combat evil and injustice through martial-arts moves and through huge space-travel-like and robotic-looking vehicles with lots of special powers. Their adversaries are typically Japanimation-type monsters and evil no-goods who are out to steal and plunder and cause havoc.

As a full-scale licensed property, *Power Rangers* is primarily a TV series and toy line, and beyond that has penetrated into virtually all other mediums, including apparel, home decor, eating utensils, home video, and feature film.

After having analyzed the different ingredients that add up to the *Power Rangers* phenomenon, observers have noted that there are seven aspects that contribute to its success:

> **A. IDENTIFICATION:** Again, it is a form of Identification—this time *Emulatory Identification*—that is of primary import when considering the "draw" that the Power Rangers Concept has on children 3 through 7. To review:
>
>> **Emulation:** In an "Emulatory" Identification Pattern the child emulates or "wants to be like" the human or animal character/object—e.g., a Batman figure, Bugs Bunny, a Barbie® doll.
>>
>> Three-through-7-year-olds—especially males—are particularly prone to hero identification or emulation. This is an age when "power" and especially powerful characters (Superman, Batman, GIJoe, the X-Men) are particularly attractive because after all, the 3-through-7-year-old is a little person without much power in a world of giant adults who wield a great deal of power over him.
>
> **B. POWER AND CONTROL:** This brings up the whole issue of *power* or *control.* It is our view that control or power is a fundamental need of human beings in that without power over our environment we would not survive. In our investigations we have isolated six different forms of power, which are listed below.

1. Physical power	Any use of the body or physical extensions of the body (e.g., weapons) to dominate or control
2. Intellectual power	Any use of one's mind or intelligence or knowledge/mental skill to dominate or control
3. Social power	Any use of one's social status, wealth, influence, or ability to communicate to gain power
4. Emotional power	Any use of one's own emotions (e.g., anger, sadness) or the emotions of another (e.g., fear, guilt) to control another
5. Ethical power	Any use of moral righteousness, "shoulds" and/or "shouldn'ts," to establish oneself as "right" and the other as "wrong" and thereby dominate him
6. Spiritual power	This is actually a form of "nonpower": in many ways it might be considered the only true power, relegating all other forms to the status of force versus genuine and ultimate power.

C. EMULATION AND PHYSICAL POWER: From the above list it should be clear that it is primarily their *physical* power, i.e., their abilities in the martial arts, that gives the Power Rangers most of their power—and much of their attractiveness to children from 3 to 7. It could also be argued that they outsmart their enemies (*intellectual* power) and even that the Power Rangers are on the side of "the right," and therefore they *ethically* dominate their enemies, who are "wrong" or "evil" as well. From the child's perspective these are heroes they want to emulate and be like; these are superstars with powers that 3-to-7-year-olds want to have. This emulation is not merely a cognitive exercise; it entails a good deal of *Emotional* involvement on the part of the child. From a 5-year-old-boy's perspective, for example, he's "gonna be like that blue Power Ranger who knocks those alien bad guys down and saves the day."

Of particular note is the fact that there are five of these Power Rangers superheroes, and two of them are females! While females have held supportive roles in such other concepts as *He-Man* (She-Ra), *Star Wars* (Princess Leah), *Batman* (Cat Woman), and *Superman* (Lois Lane), this is the first time in TV history that females have formed part of a superhero team with such success and acceptance by both males and females. There appear to be three key reasons for this acceptance. First, the females have their own physical powers and abilities on a par with the males; second, when transformed and in costume they create a combined image of a consistently powerful team of superheroes. Finally, the fact that in their pretransformed state they are late teens or young adults engaged in such typical social interactions as listening to music, going to dances, and engaging in relationship intrigues and "tiffs" appeals to the particularly strong social/relationships interests of females.

D. DARK-SIDE APPEAL: The second aspect of the Power Rangers that has a great deal of appeal for the 3-through-7-year-old is the amount of "dark-side" Content in the form of the various villains and monsters that appear on the show. Children, especially boys, are particularly attracted to "bad guys." For example, during the heydays of Mattel's He-Man toy action figure, sales of the chief villain, Skeletor, and his bad-guy henchmen exceeded by almost 3 to 1 those of the "light-side" characters. Especially as children reach the older end of this 3-through-7 age range, they demand more "edge" or dark-side behavior from characters and stories.

E. JAPANIMATION: A third element of strong appeal—and also something that sets the Power Rangers apart as different and "cool," is its use of Japanese animation—especially segments that feature hokey dragons, monsters, and weird and outlandish animal and quasi-human villains. This is truly a "difference that makes a difference." To the adult eye, indeed even to many an 8-year-old-or-older's perception, these types of villains are not realistic and are corny—but to most of the under-7 crowd, these fantasy-based creatures are "awesome."

F. TRANSFORMATION: As you may be aware, a key aspect of the Power Rangers is that—like Clark Kent transforming into Superman, each of the Rangers transforms from an ordinary human into a Power Ranger complete with his/her own individual and distinctly colored costume, individual set of special talents, and special role within the robot-like vehicle that the Rangers command.

Transformation—whether of a toy car that transforms into a spaceship, or a character that transforms from one form to another—has a particularly powerful impact on the 3-through-7-year old. The child below approximately 8 years old does not yet have the cognitive sophistication of the 8+ year-old and this limits his ability to see and discern the beginning, middle, and end of a transformation process and hold it in his mind all at once. A transformational event, therefore, appears magical to him and has a great deal of surprise impact.

After approximately the age of 7, the child's brain is developing sufficiently so that he/she can, in a sense, see behind the curtain and know that X has changed to Y but still remains X "really." The 7+ year-old will still enjoy transformations but will "know the trick," so to speak. He will also demand more and more sophisticated transformations in order to be impressed.

G. TECHNOLOGY AND THE "MAGIC" OF SPECIAL EFFECTS: A final aspect that has power (again, especially for males, who have been shown to be more object-oriented than females, who are more people-and-relationships oriented) is the amount of technology that is present in a *Power Rangers* show: lasers, computers, buttons, switches, and futuristic devices. Special effects such as the Power Rangers vanishing in a flash of light or being "beamed up" in *Star Trek* style have added impact on the 3-through-7-year-old, given his/her less sophisticated cognitive processes.

It is YMS's considered view that these seven elements are the core reasons why the Power Rangers have achieved megahit status: hero identification, control, physical power, dark-side appeal, japanimation, transformation, and technology and special effects.

TRANSITIONING AWAY FROM THE CHILDISH

As intensely as children seem to get deeply involved with a phenomenon such as the Power Rangers—with Power Rangers room decor, Halloween costumes, toys, games, books, and cartoon shows—it sometimes appears mysterious why all of a sudden children move away from these concepts. Almost overnight many a 5- or 6-year-old, who just the day before couldn't live without the next Power Rangers whatever to enter the marketplace, now hides his Ranger figures under his bed and proclaims, "Aw, they're for little kids."

The *Barney & Friends* phenomenon is of particular interest here. Why is it that there has been such a "Barney backlash"? Why has it become "in" in some circles to "hate Barney"—to the point where people in Barney suits appearing in mall promotions have actually been beaten up?

The answer lies in the mentality of a 4- or 5-year-old compared to that of an individual who is growing out of his "babyish" or childhood years, i.e., a child aged 7 or older. As the 7+ year-old moves out of his previous stage of development, he typically doesn't just smoothly shift into an older period of development while continuing to be public about his love for the icons of his childish period: Mr. Rogers, Barney, Mickey Mouse, the Power Rangers. No, on the contrary, as part of establishing his "grown-up" identity and autonomy, he "disassociates" himself from them. He needs to make the things of childhood "wrong"; after all, they are "for babies" or "for little kids." He not only grows into his next period of development, he actively *pushes away* from those things associated with the earlier period.

This "push-away" phenomenon explains a great deal about the likes and dislikes of the 7+ year-old. By approximately the age of 6 or 7, children are becoming very aware of what's considered "cool" and what's not. Just let little Joey wear a pair of Tweety-Bird sneakers to school in the first grade and see the ridicule he'll attract.

Now, one would think that as the child grows out of this "sensitive" 3-through-7 period and into his/her preteens, teens, and adulthood, he/she would lose the need to make childish things such as Barney "wrong." Not the case, unfortunately. Many, it appears, are "stuck" in earlier patterns somehow and in their lack of self-confidence still need to make Barney and other simple and innocent icons wrong.

COMMON DENOMINATORS FOR SUCCESS

We've just explored the power behind two TV and toy concepts that have been megahits with the 3-through-7 age group. One could name "winning, successful products" from a great variety of other categories, such as Flintstones vitamins, Winnie the Pooh shampoo, M&M's candies, Garfield, *Casper* movies, *The Lion King* and other Disney movies, Math Blaster software, SpaghettiOs, and McDonald's Big Macs and Happy Meals.

In order to get at the common denominators that are propelling 3-through-7-year-olds toward these products and programs as well as many others, we have to take a close look—as we did for the birth-through-2-year-olds—at what's going on with them developmentally on a variety of fronts.

CORE DEVELOPMENTAL ASPECTS

The following list sets forth the core aspects of the development of the 3-through-7-year-old child.

Cognition	Prelogical, Intuitive, Bipolar, Preoperational
Neurology	R System—Brain Stem (0–7)
	M System—Limbic (1–11)
	Right Hemi—Cortex (4–15)
Perception	Centration, anthropomorphism, fantasy, overcuing
Needs/Wants	Physiological needs, love, safety, autonomy
Moral sense	Preconventional
Self/Social	Self-centered, self-protective, impulsive, independent
Humor	Slapstick, silly, action, sudden surprise, high sensory

Now let's examine each of the above aspects more closely.

NEUROLOGY

According to Joseph Chilton Pearce,[3] brain development during this 3-through-7 stage essentially focuses on three key parts of the brain:

R System—Brain Stem: 0–7	This is the most basic, most primitive part of the brain that controls autonomic functions such as the heart and breathing. Its development is focused upon from before birth through approximately 7 years of age, at which time it is essentially complete in its development.
M System—Limbic/Midbrain: 1–11	From approximately one year of age through the age of 11 the midbrain, which is among other things a core element of the emotional development and the imagination, is being "entrained" or "mapped in."
C System—Cortex, Right Hemisphere: 4–15	Starting at approximately 4 years of age and continuing through age 15, the right brain, which specializes in nonlinear, nonlogical abilities, such as visuospatial acuity and music, is being emphasized developmentally.

IMPLICATIONS

The above facts regarding the developing brain of the 3-to-7-year-old have enormous implications for product and program development. It all starts with the brain; a child's cognitive abilities, abilities of perception and the "way" he perceives, his socialization process—it is all made possible and is shaped by his developing brain's capacities along the way.

For the 3-through-7-year-old, of most importance is the fact that this age child (except for the individual at the top of this range, the 7-year-old, whose brain development is more advanced) does not yet have full left-brain cognitive abilities in place.

PACKAGING: On packaging, for example, this age child is not going to pay much, if any, attention to verbal messages, and to the extent that he might, this age child will not be very "logical" or "evaluative" in his approach to the words; he will typically accept them at face value. Visual detail is far more important for this age child. *In addition, and very importantly, because of his brain development stage, the below-7-year-old is likely to "centrate" or fixate on a predominant or other-*

wise interesting and involving stimulus to the exclusion of exploration of the whole visual field. A character or glittery heart symbol, for example, may grab and hold this young child's attention over any other graphics on the package. (See "Centration" and "Overcuing" in the section on Perception later in this chapter.)

ACCUMULATING VERSUS COLLECTING: Serious "collecting," e.g., of Barbie dolls, GIJoe figures, baseball cards, is not yet the motivation or the practice and this is also due to this "not-yet-logical" cognitive stage of the 3-through-7-year-old. Before approximately the age of 7, "collecting" is more a matter of "accumulating." More is better to the 3-through-7-year-old and this age child wants "lots of stuff."

It's important to note that most serious collecting for the 7+ age child is of "realistic" concepts rather than fantasy-based concepts. Young GIJoe collectors, for example, become as immersed in the details of the GIJoe characters' descriptions on the back of the GIJoe collector cards as they are interested in the characters' pictures or the toy action figures themselves. It is this older child's ability to discriminate and make distinctions between this character and that, between this Barbie doll and that, between this American League pitcher and that, which allows for serious collecting as opposed to simply accumulating a mass of objects.

COGNITION

A child's neurological development allows for his cognitive development or abilities with thinking. In terms of his cognitive abilities, the 3-through-7-year-old is:

Prelogical	He is not yet able to think things completely through in a logical manner. He is not yet analytical in his approach to the world but more spontaneous and illogical. His ability to think in linear fashion or sequentially—first this, then this, then that, etc.—is not yet fully in place.
Intuitive	He is impulsive and reactive rather than intellectual in his approach to the world.
Bipolar	He thinks in blacks and whites, good and bad, without much ability to discern or appreciate subtleties or the gray shades in between.
Preoperational	This Piagetian term that means the 3-to-7-year old still has problems with certain mental operations such as "reversibility."

The thinking and processing of the 3-through-7-year-old changes dramatically from that of the infant/toddler of the previous birth-through-age-

2-sensorimotor period, primarily because it is no longer restricted to immediate perceptual and motor events. Thought at this stage of development is now representational (symbolic) and behavior sequences can be played out in the child's head rather than only in real physical events. Language is acquired very rapidly between the ages of 2 and 4 years. Many behaviors in the early part of this period are often egocentric rather than social.

As the child approaches 6 and 7 years of age, however, language, behavior, and communication become more and more social. However, the thought-processing of the 3-through-7-year-old is still restricted in many ways. The first limitation is that thought proceeds in one direction only (nonreversibility). This means that the child often cannot retrace her thinking process back to where it started. This creates a prelogical period of thought which is largely under the control of the immediate environment and therefore is driven by environmental stimuli. The net result is a child who is impulsive and reactive in her approach to the world, more than logical, reasonable, or reflective.

IMPLICATIONS

This 3-through-7 prelogical period of development allows for great flexibility in the child's world. Fantasy abounds. Virtually anything is possible in the child's mind. A stick can become a snake, a rock, a turtle; and a tree can be a monster in the imagination of this young child. This way of thinking is referred to as *anthropomorphism,* in which nonhuman objects are given human characteristics. Entertainment forms such as TV and film programming therefore can stretch the limits of reality way beyond what a 7+ year-old, with his more logical faculties, might be able to bear.

This prelogical period—along with the child's needs for love and stimulation—also accounts in part for the strong affinity to animals and animal characters found at this young developmental stage. The child can identify or connect with these objects because she can easily attribute human qualities to them, making them symbolically important. The child categorizes language, however, in dichotomies or what many refer to as "Black-or-White thinking." Once something has taken on a particular frame of reference in the child's mind, it is categorized or given its meaning; it takes time developmentally for it to become symbolic of something else at the same time. This narrow and structured type of thought is gradually transformed toward the end of this developmental period.

Of further significance in relation to the above discussion is the power of "light-side" versus "dark-side" objects and characters. The child in the prelogical stage will easily dichotomize concepts into polarities. This applies to characters, who are viewed as either "good" or "bad." In the entertainment medium simple polarized characteristics and their "cues," e.g., Superman-type cape for a hero and an evil face or an eye patch for a villain, are utilized in the development of characters and character dynamics.

PERCEPTION

It is useful to visualize how the 3-to-7-year-old "looks at" or perceives the world. The following "filter" model illustrates the 3-through-7-year-old's perceptual window on the world. Figure 5.1 shows this model

FIGURE 5.1: A MODEL OF THE PERCEPTUAL FILTER OF THE 3-THROUGH-7-YEAR-OLD

Because of his neurological and cognitive stage of development, the 3-through-7-year-old perceives the world quite distinctly from children older than this age range, and most certainly quite differently from adults. For example, there are a variety of developmental "principles" besides anthropomorphism that play a significant role in how children between 3 and 7 process information: centration, overcuing, fantasy, and egocentrism.

IMPLICATIONS

A. CENTRATION: Centration refers to the child's perceptual process of centering or fixing attention on only a limited dimension or perceptual aspect of the visual stimulus that is encountered. In other words, this younger child often is unable to "explore" all aspects of the visual stimulus, or "decenter" her visual inspection. On a toy item such as a large doll, for example, the child on first sight may "centrate" on only one aspect of the doll, such as the big shiny red bow. This can be so compelling to the child's attention that other less visually predominant aspects of the doll are simply overlooked, and the child's preferencing goes to the doll with the bow rather than some other more expensive doll that has a variety of more subtle features—which are appreciated only by an older child's or adult's eye.

This very thing occurred not too long ago at YMS Consulting, when we were conducting some qualitative testing of a large-doll concept with 5-through-8-year-old girls. The toy manufacturer had spent a gazillion dollars on the sculpting of a refined and beautiful realistic doll's face and on a play feature that they hoped would be a "difference that makes a difference"—the doll went from a lying-on-her-back position to a sitting position with the push of a button. There were two competing dolls in the test, however—one a $50.00 doll with beautiful face and dress, and another a $19.95 doll with a huge, shiny, bright red sequined heart sewn on her dress. Guess which one was preferred by three out of four of the girls: the one with the sequined heart. This shiny and attractive symbol became an object of centration that captured and held the attention of most of the girls to the exclusion of all other attributes.

B. OVERCUING: Overcuing is related to centration, in that a certain dimension of the stimulus, if oversized or exaggerated, "grips" the child in a centrating type of response and becomes the predominant feature of the stimulus that attracts the child. A big shiny red bow atop a doll's head, for example, may dominate the visual field, and the child will "fixate" or "centrate" on it to the exclusion of other visual stimuli. An action figure's muscles, such as those of the He-Man action figures or the World Wrestling Federation WWF action figures, is also a clear case of overcuing.

C. MAGICAL/FANTASY THINKING: Magical thinking is related to the emphasis on right-hemisphere brain development. This 3-to-approximately-6-or-7 stage of growth is a period of concentration on or "mapping in" of the right brain's development. With this type of neurology predominant, the child is naturally engaged in imagination and play as a means of defining his world and creating the foundations for the next stage of development. Less magical/fantasy thinking will predominate, and logical cognitive operations will follow, at approximately 7 years of age, when the left hemisphere of the cortex unfolds as the primary focus of brain development.

D. EGOCENTRISM: According to Piaget,[4] self-centeredness is a natural stage of development that correlates with the different stages of intellectual growth. At each new stage of mental growth, the child's ability to differentiate and understand another's point of view expands and assumes a unique form, expressed through a newly developed set of behaviors. The 3-through-7-year-old child (especially 3 through 5) does not yet possess strong abilities to understand and integrate another's point of view. The self-centeredness of this period subsides as social interaction with others (particularly peers) increases. By the end of this developmental period, the child is able to begin to see and take into account another's point of view.

NEEDS

PHYSIOLOGICAL NEEDS

Basic physical needs such as shelter, food, and protection from harm (safety) are still very important during this period, along with the needs for love and stimulation. This stimulation need partially accounts for the "busyness" of this developmental period, as children this age are still naturally very curious about life and ready to explore its many aspects. Since they are not yet encumbered with logical, analytical thought, they are able to be free in their explorations, accepting fantastic explanations as readily as real ones. The attention span of these up-to-7-year-olds is more variable and defocused when it comes to abstract stimuli, but there is nothing inherently limited in their attention spans when it comes to naturally exploring what has interest for them.

LOVE

The 3-through-7-year-old is very much in need of love. The bonding and trust process is still very much in development during these early years, and, when successfully established, forms a solid emotional foundation for the child as he enters the sometimes not-so-safe worlds of school, the playground, and his peers.

AUTONOMY

Importantly at this stage of development a child's need for autonomy—that is, the beginnings of separation from his parents—emerges during this period and is the beginning of a growing independence that, in healthy situations, doesn't fully complete itself until the late teens and sometimes even early adulthood. This need for autonomy also translates into an attraction toward and "identification"—especially on the part of males—with powerful characters, adults, heroes, villains, archetypes with powers of all kinds. It could be said that because this is a period of not having much personal power (the adults in a 3-through-7-year-old's life wield great power over him) power and powerful figures become very attractive and invite emulation.

IMPLICATIONS

The needs of a 3-through-7-year-old have great implications for product and program development and marketing.

THE NEED FOR STIMULATION: Leads to the 3-through-7-year-old's insatiable desire to be busy and entertained, whether it be via free and spontaneous play alone or with others, via film, TV, game-playing, toys, and learning experiences.

THE NEED FOR LOVE: Accounts for a child of this age's positive response to animals of all kinds, especially safe ones such as domestic animals and baby animals—even stuffed animals.

THE NEED FOR SAFETY: Reminds us that this age child still needs to feel safe and in a protected environment that he can trust. To take a 3-to-5-year-old to a scary movie such as *Jurassic Park* or *Jumanji,* for example, would not serve the best interests of this age child's need to feel safe.

THE NEED FOR AUTONOMY: Is this age child's growing need for power and independence. He will, therefore, be attracted—perhaps more than at other stages of development—to such figures of power as fantasy superheroes and sports stars.

THE MORAL SENSE

Kohlberg characterizes the 3-through-7-year-old's moral development stage as "preconventional."[5] This means essentially that this age child hasn't yet formed an advanced morality, or sense of good/bad, right/wrong for himself independent of the values of the adults in his life. He accepts in most cases what he is told in regard to morality.

IMPLICATIONS

Adults have a responsibility to be careful about the "shoulds" and "shouldn'ts," the "rights" and "wrongs" that they are inculcating into these young minds. Although it is a natural socialization process for adults to "teach" the young what's good and bad, great care must be taken so that children are left empowered. Children of this stage of development are particularly vulnerable to what is being taught by superheroes, for example, whether they be Power Rangers or World Wrestling Federation stars. If these fantasy heroes "teach"—through their actions—violent resolution of conflict, for example, this is exactly what children can adopt as their own code of ethics and behavior. "After all, that's how the superhero did it!"

SELF/SOCIAL DEVELOPMENT

The 3-through-7-year-old as a social being is largely *self-centered, self-protective,* and *impulsive.* In terms of this child's emerging development of "self" and his interrelationships with others, he is primarily self-oriented or egocentric, with the world revolving around *him.* He is impulsive rather than logical or thoughtful about his wants and decision-making, and is growing in his sense of independence.

IMPLICATIONS

When a child below the age of about 5 plays, she will often tend to "parallel play" rather than fully play cooperatively and interactively with others in her peer group—although girls will tend to play cooperatively with others earlier than boys. For example, if two 4-year-olds are playing dolls together, they will typically each play more in their own "world" and by themselves rather than interact much with a playmate, who is playing in her own world right alongside. This is not a rule but a tendency. A product or program designer, therefore, would do well to take care not to design products or programs that require too much intentional interaction or cooperation among playmates for this younger end of the 3-through-7 age range.

HUMOR

Primarily because of cognitive and therefore perceptual limitations, children of this age group are not yet ready intellectually for advanced forms of humor such as puns, word play, innuendo, sarcasm, and satire. More appropriate forms of humor for the 3-through-7-year-old are *slapstick, action, sudden surprise,* and *high sensory/physical* forms of humor. What is perceived to be funny by a child of this age group is very much delimited by his cognitive abilities. Since his mental abilities do not yet include the ability to adequately see the "gray" in things, and since abstract reasoning is not yet in place, forms of humor that depend on higher cognitive functioning such as innuendo, sarcasm, puns, and word play are most often lost on this age child. Children at this developmental stage respond strongly to visual forms of humor, especially high-action slapstick humor that is more physical/sensory than cerebral. The slapstick, pie- (or brick-) in-the-face type of humor seen in the movie *Home Alone* is a good example of this type.

IMPLICATIONS

Humor for the 3-through-7-year age range should focus on high-action, sensory, physical, slapstick types of humor. Superiority types of humor such as name-calling and "put-downs" are also funny to this age group, but should be utilized with sensitivity. The implications for product and program developers are important—stay away from focusing on forms of humor that are too sophisticated and that require advanced cognitive ability.

Note that many forms of entertainment are "layered" in that they simultaneously provide certain types of humor such as slapstick for the younger segment of their audience while providing more subtle forms of humor for older viewers. A typical *Bugs Bunny* episode, for example, will include lots of pie-in-the-face humor, such as his nemesis Elmer Fudd falling into a pit, but Bugs will also make sarcastic, cutting remarks that sometimes are quite sophisticated. Among other things, this accounts for Bugs Bunny's broad appeal across a wide spectrum of age groups. It is a "filters" phenomenon. If I am 5 years old and watching Bugs, I see through my more limited 3-through-7 filter. And if I am older, I see Bugs through a filter that is expanded, and that includes the ability to discern and appreciate humor of a wider variety, including more abstract forms.

SUMMARY

By way of summary, let's revisit the YMS Product Leverage Matrix and briefly highlight the most critical aspects of the Matrix in relation to the 3-to-7-year-old along with additional winning products and programs:

A. CONCEPT: This age child will become most attracted to and involved with concepts that are a match with his 3-through-7 developmental stage of development. For example, these will be concepts that are not overly abstract, concepts that do not require sophisticated reasoning power. (Again, toward the top end of this 3-through-7 age range, children will begin to relate to more complicated concepts.) There are so many concepts from so many different product categories that there is insufficient space to discuss all of them. Here are some examples, however.

FIGURE 5.2: THE PRODUCT LEVERAGE MATRIX

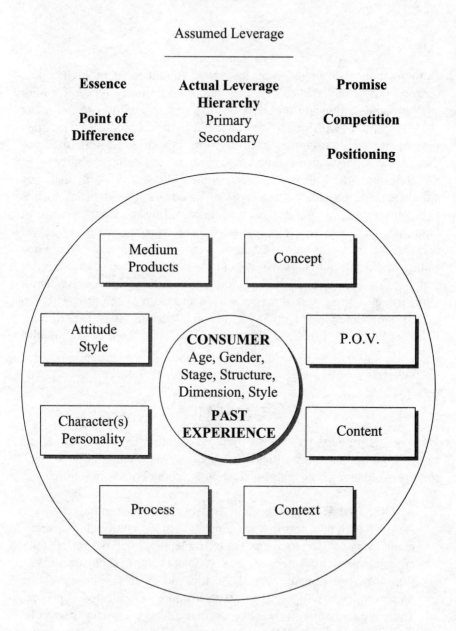

© 1997 YMS Consulting/Innertainment Inc.

Games: Simpler board games or card games, such as Hi-Ho! Cherry-O, Chutes & Ladders, and UNO, rather than games that require more advanced calculation or reasoning, such as Monopoly, Scrabble, Clue, or poker.

Toys: Virtually all toys are right on target for the 3-to-7-year-old stage. In fact, toy companies are constantly challenged in attempting to expand the appeal of their toys upward beyond the age of 7 or 8. Certainly children 8+ do buy and play with "toys" but these toys must now be "age-appropriate," meaning they must provide the 8+ child with "older" play patterns. Electronic games certainly fit within this parameter, given their level of sophistication, complexity, and difficulty.

B. PROCESS: *Process* refers to "technical" aspects of products and programs, such as music, special effects, and the pacing or speed at which stimuli are presented. The critical thing to keep in mind here is simplicity as opposed to complexity. Children 3 through 7 require relatively simple and straightforward approaches to such things as special effects and music. And especially the younger end of this age spread—3-through-5-year-olds—respond better to relatively slower pacing (e.g., in TV advertising/programming) compared to 7+ year-olds.

C. CHARACTERS: Children of this developmental period will also relate positively to most cartoon characters which are age-appropriate: all the Disney characters, the Warner Brothers line-ups including the Looney Tunes gang led by Bugs Bunny, and Spielberg's Animaniacs. They will not yet relate (thank goodness) as readily to more abstract, excessively dark or complicated and vapid characters such as Duckman, the Simpsons, and Beavis and Butt-Head. Kids toward the top of this age range (i.e., 5+) will also begin to "push away" from excessively babyish characters, such as Barney and some of the Sesame Street crew.

Crossover Characters: There are a few characters, such as Tasmanian Devil, Bugs Bunny, and Garfield that have strong appeal for a broad spectrum of ages—both this 3-through-7-year-old period of development and the next, or 8-through-12, stage. This is essentially a "filters" phenomenon. In other words, the 3-through-7-year-old, looking through *her* filter, sees in Garfield, for example, a mischievous, cute cat, and this is sufficient even though she may not yet comprehend the edgier subtleties of his character, such as his sarcasm. The 8+ year-old, however, now has more abstract cognitive abilities, which allow her to look through a more complex filter, if you will, and which allows her to appreciate a wider range of Garfield's personality and humor.

D. CONTEXT: *Context* refers to both time period and sociogeographical locale. Children of this developmental stage, since they do not yet have sophisticated cognitive abilities in place, relate best to "now" time orientations and do not respond as well typically to historical (past-based) or to future-based concepts. Sociogeographically, they also respond best to social locales that are close to home rather than foreign or outer-space settings.

FROM FANTASY TO REALITY

By now you should have a solid understanding of the 3-through-7-year-old and his or her capabilities, as well as a solid sense of what drives his/her attention and involvement. In the next chapter, we move from the "fantasy" stage into the "reality" stage of development. There are a great many shifts and changes to account for in the child's evolution.

CHAPTER 6

AGES 8 THROUGH 12
The Rule/Role Stage

> Children have never been very good at listening to their
> elders, but they have never failed to imitate them.
> —James Baldwin,
> *Nobody Knows My Name*[1]

Preadolescents. Preteens. Tweens. By whatever name, the 8-through-12-year-old finds herself in a brain growth period characterized by a neurological focus on the development of the left brain. And in her social development, among many other tasks, this preteen is starting to look at and define for herself what it takes to get along in the world.

A child this age is quite impressionable and is quick to attach herself to celebrity and sports "heroes" and other role models such as teachers, parents, and church leaders. It is because of this age child's thirst for discovering reality or "what's so" and discerning the right things to do and the right things to become that this period is referred to as the "Rule/Role" stage of development.

A NEW FOCUS IN BRAIN DEVELOPMENT

Most important to note regarding this developmental stage is a major shift in the focus of brain development at approximately 6 or 7 years of age. Before this age the 3-through-6-year-old was stretching and expanding his imaginative muscles through a more concentrated "mapping in" of the right brain—which continues through the 8-through-12 stage but takes a "back burner" to the left brain's development. At approximately age 6 or 7 the development of the left brain and of its intellect, logic, and reasoning capacities takes center stage.

If you've ever wondered why it is that children at about the age of 6 or 7 start to leave behind many of their more "childish" activities and objects, a central factor is this shift from a right-brain developmental focus to an emphasis on a left-brain focus.

It is widely known that the cortex, or "higher brain," is vertically divided into two halves or hemispheres, each with its own specializations. The gray matter (cortex) of the right half of the brain is primarily responsible for visuospatial tasks, artistic development, music, and emotional activity. The left brain, on the other hand—or "on the other brain" so to speak—becomes specialized in reasoning, logic, math, and analytical activity with language and numbers.

There is a great deal of complexity to the dynamics of the functions of the left and right hemispheres of the brain. Many people tend to oversimplify, for example, when they argue for a clean differentiation between the hemispheres. General statements like "the right hemisphere is the imaginative brain and the left hemisphere is the logical brain" are gross oversimplifications. Suffice it to say, however, that there is general agreement that each hemisphere has its specializations.

In fact, toward the end of this stage at around the age of 11, Joseph Chilton Pearce suggests, there is a neural "housecleaning," so to speak, that dissolves all unmyelinated neural fields in order to increase the efficiency of the brain. Millions of unmyelinated neurons are literally swept out of existence.[2] The years 8 through 12, therefore, are highly critical to the child's development. In *Evolution's End,* Pearce states that the first five to six years of life have served to establish key "structures of knowledge" of the self, the world, and language:

> By around age six this fundamental world-self-language system is complete, and nature turns to the development of her latest addition, the neocortex, ushering us into the world of intellect, logic and reasoning. . . . [T]he six-year-old still has a potential (neural) field capacity vastly greater than it had earlier or will have later. Estimates of neurons in our brain range to as many as a hundred billion. Obviously an infinite number of possible neural fields and an unlimited possibility for translating potential into actuality is inherent within that six-year-old's head.

This neocortical developmental focus has critical implications for product and program development as well as marketing and advertising to kids in this 8-through-12 age range. This child is no longer a primarily fantasy-oriented child; this child is fast developing and exercising logical reasoning skills that disallow previous forms of play and activity and which open up more "left-brain"-oriented activities and challenges.

This is not to say that fantasy goes away at age 7. God knows even we adults certainly indulge in and engage in fantasy throughout life. Witness the popularity of soap operas, for example. The *type* of fantasy changes at around 7, however. Before this age the child is center-stage in a more magical period of development in which anything is possible and logical rules are not necessary. Trees can talk, Barney is a real purple dinosaur (not a person in a dinosaur suit), and Santa and the Easter Bunny are genuine entities. Around age 6 or 7 these childish fantasies begin to go by the wayside and are replaced by more "realistic" fantasies if you will—fantasies based on at least somewhat plausible possibilities such as *Star Wars, Jurassic Park,* or *ER,* or fantasies as they occur in romance novels and fiction.

Why does the Barbie® fashion-doll line continue its appeal beyond 8? Part of the answer lies in "realism" versus "fantasy." Unlike such fantasy-doll concepts as the Strawberry Shortcake or My Little Pony toy lines, Barbie® is based on a "real" girl who is approximately in her late teens or early twenties. This sets up an emulatory identification pattern in which 3- to approximately 13-year-olds want to "be like" Barbie—pretty and successful. For boys, GIJoe is a similar model. Compared to a fantasy-based action-figure toy concept such as the very successful (with 3-through-6-year-olds) He-Man Masters of the Universe line, the GIJoe action-figure line is based in reality, that is, it is based on real military vehicles and characters of the United States military. Both these concepts also take advantage of the 8+ child's love for collecting—and now this collecting has moved beyond simple accumulation and into serious collecting complete with this older child's cognitive abilities that allow discernment and differentiation between, for example, action figures, collector cards, and Barbie doll costumes, all of which require a good deal of attention to detail.

THE BIG "PUSH AWAY"

It's very important to note that as children transition out of the "right-brain"–dominated 3-through-7 stage of development, they don't typically just leave the things of childhood behind. In order to be perceived by themselves and others as "growing up" (peer acceptance and opinion enter in at this stage as potent forces), *they often feel the need to aggressively "push away" from more childish concepts* such as Power Rangers, Barney, *Sesame Street,* or "playing with dolls" or fantasy-based action figures. They may even feel the need to make these childish concepts "wrong" in order to establish themselves as "beyond them." For example, you might hear them say, "That's for little kids!"

To psychologize for just a moment: many teens and adults seem to have unwarranted intense aversions for some of these childishly simple characters such as Barney. Could it be that some people haven't quite been able to establish strong enough self identities, so they feel the need to affirm themselves by putting Barney and Mickey Mouse and Mr. Rogers down? Barney and Mickey and his gang and *Mr. Rogers' Neighborhood* and other soft and simple programs and characters are ideal for the 3-through-6 stage of development. As children move out of this stage, however, it is time (except for nostalgic and collecting purposes) for them to leave the things of their early childhood behind.

PREADOLESCENT WINNERS

There are a great many products and programs that have achieved "winner" status in recent times with the 8-through-12-year-old. Studied closely, it is easy to see that these winners are characterized by much more complexity and left-brain involvement, and more realistic themes than those found attractive by the 3-through-7-year-old. Some winners with 8-through-12-year-olds include the following products.

SPORTS ITEMS: This age group loves sports. From Nerf Balls to squirt guns to sports equipment to sports-related clothing to sports-themed video games to actually participating in all kinds of sports, sports offer variety, challenge, competition, and just plain fun.

COLLECTOR CARDS: The 8-through-12-year-old, because of his move away from fantasy and toward realism, and because his logical abilities are fast developing, becomes very interested in collector cards. His interest includes all the minute details on the backs of these cards: details about sports figures, GIJoe characters, and comic-book characters such as the X-Men. Collecting, comparing, swapping, buying and selling—these are all very engaging activities for this age group—and for males more than females.

PUBLICATIONS: A variety of publications from comic books to kid-targeted magazines such as *Disney Adventures* magazine, to Barbie® publications, to video-games publications such as *Nintendo Power,* capture the attention of the 8-through-12-year-old. Not only does this type of reading fit a more left-brain orientation, but these publications are filled with a variety of role models to emulate.

TV SHOWS AND MOVIES: The types of TV shows and movies that most appeal to the 8-through-12-year-old are essentially comedic and action-oriented. For example, most of the formula sitcoms that proliferate on TV tubes, as well as such animation as the *Animaniacs, Bugs Bunny,* and *Road Runner,* off-the-wall and gross types of TV shows such as *The Ren & Stimpy Show,* the latest outrageous Jim Carrey film offering, and action programs and films such as are starred in by the likes of Arnold Schwarzenegger, Bruce Willis, Jean-Claude Van Damme, and Sylvester Stallone find a receptive audience in this age group.

MEGAHITS

Now, let's take a closer look at two play activities that have achieved megahit status with the 8-through-12-year-old.

ELECTRONIC GAMES

No other category of product has achieved such blockbuster success with the 8-through-12-year-olds as video games and computer games. It's important to note that boys are more avid game-players than girls, who account for only approximately 20 percent of electronic game play. For this age group electronic games provide six types of play and involvement that really pay off.

A. CHALLENGE: Many electronic games take weeks to "beat," that is, to completely master all the "screens" and levels of difficulty. Much of this challenge is mechanical: training one's finger dexterity, speed, and sensorimotor processing skills. However, there are many games that require logic and inductive and deductive reasoning to figure out, and this is very stimulating and challenging.

B. COMPETITION: Many electronic games—especially sports, racing, and fighting games—are designed such that the player is pitted either against another game-player opponent or opponents, or against the computer. This head-to-head or player-against-the-computer competition is very involving and can be quite exciting.

C. COMPLEXITY: Compared to traditional toys such as action figures, model airplanes, Frisbees, and dolls, electronic games have an inherent complexity that is rich in variety of visual and auditory stimulation. This high level of complexity creates and demands a high degree of interactivity that is very engrossing and challenging—to the point of total absorption on the part of the child, in many cases.

D. REWARD: Inherent in every electronic game by virtue of its design is the fact that at almost every point throughout a game the electronic-game player is receiving positive reinforcement. Move the mouse to the right—and the computer screen responds with a game movement that the player "caused." Shoot at a target and make a "hit"—and he is rewarded. Throw a touchdown pass—and there's a reward. The game player is constantly being reinforced and rewarded for his actions; this is highly motivating and stimulating.

E. STIMULATION: Compared to traditional toys, electronic games provide a great deal of visual and auditory stimulation: the roar of racing cars or flying jets, the fun musical background sounds to Pac-Man or Sonic the Hedgehog, the roar of the crowd in an NBA Jam basketball game. These constantly changing sights and sounds are very engaging.

F. VARIETY: The electronic-games category is also a winner with the 8-through-12 target because of the great variety of games available. There are simple adaptations of board games such as computer chess, there are sports games including just about every sport imaginable from football to Ping-Pong, there are racing games, flying games, roleplay games, fighting games, and puzzle-like games. This variety represents an extremely enticing menu of possibilities to the preteen.

THE FUTURE OF ELECTRONIC GAMES: There is nothing to indicate a slowdown in children's involvement in video games, whether they utilize one of the many game hardware systems such as Nintendo, Sega, and Sony are constantly developing, or games designed for the computer. Complexity, challenge, and variety are hard to beat for the 8+ year-old as fundamental aspects of an entertainment genre. In the future this category will likely only become more flexible with more variety and challenge. Within only a few years the typical household TV set will behave more like an interactive TV/computer/game system/telephone than its current, relatively passive soon-to-be-ancestor. Stimulation, interactivity, challenge, highspeed movement, sound-effects, competition, and variety—these attributes of electronic games are intensely attractive and involving to the preadolescent as well as to many other age groups, and the proof is in their winning results at retail.

MEGA MEGA BARBIE®, BARBIE

Many toy companies have crashed and burned over the past decades because they didn't have the steady income base that is provided by a megahit "staple" like Barbie. In recent times, Barbie® sales accounted for a large portion of Mattel Incorporated's income—around a billion dollars a year. Many doll concepts are rejected by 8-through-12-year-olds as "for younger than me"; what is it about Barbie that accounts for her huge success year after year—not only for the below-age-8 girl, but continuing into the 8-through-12 stage of development? In our view, there are six key elements that account for the winner status of the Barbie doll.

A. EMULATION: In the previous chapter, in our discussion of the success of the Cabbage Patch Kids dolls, we outlined four different ways kids relate to such entities as dolls, action figures, characters, movie and TV stars. There was Nurturing Identification, "Like Me" Identification, Emulatory Identification, and "Disidentification." For the Cabbage Patch Kids, Nurturing Identification was the type of identification that provided primary motivational juices.

For Barbie®, the kind of identification pattern that exists between a preteen female and Barbie and her friends is Emulation. Girls want to "be like" Barbie and her pals in some way: pretty, glamorous, popular, successful. This emulation of Barbie and her friends provides for much of the reason for Barbie's popularity—especially in a developmental stage termed the "Rule/Role" stage, in which an 8-through-12-year-old's focus is on figuring out who she is through the multitude of role models that exist in her psychocultural environment.

B. AESTHETICS: Barbie® and everything that surrounds her—from a "macro" view of the blast of shocking pink characteristic of the Barbie aisle at the local toy store to the microcosmic world of buttons and bows and lace and glimmering sequins that adorn her person—everything is beautiful. It's all somewhat garish perhaps through the eyes of an adult, but "very pretty" and "beautiful" through an 8-through-12-year-old girl's eyes. Idealistic? Yes, but so what? Aren't we all attracted to the aesthetic? For the preteen girl, the Barbie doll's beauty and the aesthetic of all that surrounds her is immensely appealing, especially as Barbie is associated with images of success that have been idealized in large portions of our culture.

C. PLAY PATTERNS: A third element of the appeal of Barbie® lies in the rich play patterns that come about through the line-up of Barbie, her doll friends, and a plethora of accessories including houses, stables, swimming pools, cars, jewelry, and of course the equivalent of doll closets filled with doll clothes. There are essentially four main play patterns: dress-up, grooming, manipulative play with Barbie accessories, and role play with other doll characters and animals. This last play pattern of role play is particularly interesting, given the 8-through-12-year-old's "Rule/Role" stage of development. Whether alone or with siblings or girlfriends, Barbie and her circle afford an opportunity to act out a whole host of relationship interactions. Is Ken going to be late to pick up Barbie for the prom? What happened that made Barbie's little sister Skipper mad at her? And on and on. Role play is a very important way for this age child to act out different relationship scenarios and learn through play.

D. SOCIAL DYNAMICS: Play with Barbie®—unlike a great many toys that are played with primarily alone—is quite often a social activity. Because so many young girls own and play with Barbie (penetration in the U.S. is over 90 percent), and because of the great variety of Barbie dolls, friend dolls, and accessories that exist, Barbie play is often a time for interactive play with others. This common interest contributes also to the great and enduring success of Barbie.

E. COLLECTING AND DISPLAY: Before the age of around 6 or 7, little girls' interest in Barbie® centers around dress-up, grooming, and less sophisticated role play. After about age 7, different emphases within play patterns emerge. For example, more elaborate and intricate forms of role play will surface as well as the phenomenon of more serious collecting rather than just accumulating lots of Barbie dolls and Barbie stuff. (This serious collecting carries on into the adult years for many women.) Because the brain is fast developing its logical capacities, distinctions between different types of Barbie dolls and Barbie friends and accessories are much more interesting and noticed. Once the ability to critically compare is in place, collecting takes on a whole new meaning and power.

Displaying one's Barbie dolls in one's room, for example, is also part of the appeal of having a "Barbie collection." Not only is it rewarding to admire and peruse the beauty of one's own Barbie collection alone, it's also fun to show off one's collection to others. Nostalgia enters into the picture as well, as young girls mature and move through the preteen years. While some 9-year-olds, for example, may begin to be a bit embarrassed about "playing Barbie" with girlfriends due to internally and externally imposed role expectations, in the privacy of their own hearts and rooms these same girls still emotionally relate to and identify with Barbie.

F. NEW AND DIFFERENT PRODUCTS: Mattel has been a stellar example within toymaker ranks in their ability to keep the Barbie® line alive and growing by creating a constant flow of new Barbie themes and accessories. This updating of the line, or line management, keeps the Barbie line-up forever fresh and new and therefore forever interesting. What will Barbie be up to next? Astronaut Barbie? Equestrian Barbie? Malibu Barbie? Cowgirl Barbie? Businesswoman Barbie? Barbie for President? You name it, Barbie's been it—short of Plumber Barbie, perhaps, or Sanitation Worker Barbie.

Add to these new roles for Barbie all types of new accessories that involve a whole new variety of play patterns—make your own color-changing Barbie jewelry, or add colorful falls to her hair, or enjoy the special $59 Christmas edition of Barbie, pink etcetera after pink etcetera, and you have a great deal of variety that creates constant interest and involvement for the Barbie consumer.

QUESTIONS OF ETHICS

Concepts and products such as electronic games or Barbie®—and many other "successes"—carry with them many times a great deal of controversy. For example, is there a downside to kids spending so much time with and getting so involved with electronic games? What about the level of violence in many games? And isn't Barbie® creating stereotypes that are not in the best interest of girls 8 through 12? The majority of this book is dedicated to determining *what works* about concepts targeted to kids at different ages and stages of development—without attention to any possible positive or negative influences these products/programs might have. However, we at YMS are concerned about these issues, as demonstrated by the fact that we have consistently refused to consult on excessively violent concepts. Issues regarding the positive and negative impact of different concepts are discussed in Chapter 2 on "Kid Empowerment."

COMMON DENOMINATORS FOR SUCCESS

As in previous chapters, in order to get at what it is that underlies the success of winning products and programs for this age segment, we must explore the different aspects of the 8-through-12-year-old's development. The list below sets forth these aspects.

Core Developmental Aspects: 8-to-12-Year-Olds		
Neurological	M-SYSTEM:	Midbrain or Limbic (ages 1 to 11)
	C-SYSTEM:	Right hemisphere: Cortex (4 to 15)
	Left hemisphere: Cortex	(7+)
Cognition	Concrete operational, Simple abstractions, Logic	
Perception	Rule/Role, Detail, "Conformity filter"	
Needs	Acceptance, Success, Role enactment, Rule learning	
Moral sense	Conventional Morality	
Self/Social	Conformist-Social and Peer Roles	
Humor	Slapstick plus Abstraction, Darkside Appeal (gross, violent, irreverent, taboo)	

Now let's examine each of these aspects in order to understand the 8-through-12-year-old, and then look at some of the implications that each of these developmental aspects has for successful product and program development targeted to this age segment.

NEUROLOGY AND COGNITION

Let's look at an overview of which aspects of the brain are engaged in which types of development during this 8-through-12 stage, and consequently how this is linked to cognition or thinking. Neurologically, the following centers of the brain are developing:

M-SYSTEM: Midbrain or Limbic (1–11)
C-SYSTEM: Right Hemisphere: Cortex (4–15)
Left Hemisphere: Cortex (7+)

As you can see, a new set of developmental skills now emerges related to a focus on the *left* hemisphere's evolution. The left hemisphere's strongest period of development begins at around age 7. Both the midbrain (sometimes referred to as the emotional brain) and the right hemisphere of the cortex continue to develop, but they take a "back burner" developmentally during this period so that the growth of the brain's logical, rational capacities can be focused upon capacities and abilities that directly result in a host of new behaviors at this developmental stage. According to Pearce, the midbrain's development essentially completes itself toward the end of this stage at around age 11.[3]

Because of these developments, the 8-through-12-year-old is now "arming herself" with cognitive/thinking tools and abilities that heretofore were only in "incubation," so to speak. In particular, at around 7 or 8 she is beginning to be able to handle simple abstractions, think more rationally and logically—i.e., in sequence: first this, then that. The ability to distinguish one thing from another and pay attention to and appreciate detail also vastly improves because of this left-brain growth and development.

IMPLICATIONS

The 8-through-12-stage left-hemisphere development focus and emphasis —along with social changes that are intertwined with these neurological/ cognitive shifts—have a variety of implications for product and program development. Let's explore a few of them to illustrate:

TOYS AND GAMES: The preteen is leaving the relatively simple, fantasy-based toys and games behind, e.g., nonmotorized toy cars, baby dolls, fantasy-based action figures, simple games (electronic, board, card), simple construction sets, and stuffed animals.

He/she is now interested in more complex, reality-based toys such as fashion dolls, collectible figures, more complex and sophisticated electronic card and board games, and sports toys. The interest is more in serious collecting rather than—as in the previous 3-through-7 stage—just accumulating lots of stuff.

Girls, for example, in the category of craft activities are moving during this stage of development beyond simple activities such as stringing beads or coloring and pasting to more complex, intricate, and challenging craft activities such as sewing, jewelry design, and sculpting.

TV AND FILM: Newly developing neural structures and cognitive abilities allow the preadolescent to follow more sophisticated plots. (In the previous 3-through-7 stage, children were very "now" oriented and were not prepared developmentally to relate well to past or future time orientations. The younger child is also not yet able to grasp sophisticated sequences and see how beginning, middle, and end all work together. And most certainly children in the younger end of the 3-through-7 age range would have difficulty following a series of intertwined subplots in a TV show or movie.) The child aged 8 or above, however, quickly tires of stories that are excessively simple and in fact demands more complexity.

Humor in the media: It's no accident that the types of cutting and edgy humor inherent in *Bugs Bunny* episodes or *Animaniacs,* or *Garfield,* or Jim Carrey-type slapstick appeals strongly to this age. The 8-through-12-year-old's cognitive abilities allow for understanding and appreciating such humor. One of the reasons why this type of "irreverent" humor works so well with this age group is that they are in the stage of development we call the "Rule/Role" stage. This is a period of "trying to do the right thing" and "fitting in." Unconsciously, therefore, there is a need during this time for what might be called a "dark-side outlet"—and darker, edgier, irreverent forms of humor such as gross jokes, characters defeating and humiliating other characters, and characters getting the best of authority figures such as parents or teachers hit the bullseye in fulfilling this need.

It is also no accident that this preteen will prefer light TV sitcoms and lighter drama such as *Superman* to heavier drama. Especially preferred are those programs that are family-based or relationship-based, such as *Fresh Prince of Bel Air* and *Friends,* given the Rule/Role stage of development that this age child finds himself in. This age child is eager to discover and learn the rules and roles of how to get along in society.

Heavier drama such as *NYPD Blue,* by contrast, is filled with characters and content that is much more adult in its thematic appeal. Again it's largely a question of identification—finding aspects of the characters that are either like oneself, or aspects one aspires to emulate—and more sophisticated adult dramas are simply beyond the ken of most 8-through-12-year-olds.

APPAREL: Now that this age child has the cognitive tools to notice the distinctions, he will use that ability to differentiate between different brands of apparel and their attributes. When a 3-through-7-year-old sees a sneaker, he notices only salient attributes such as characters or brightly colored laces or lights that flash with each step. The brand of sneaker doesn't start to become important until the top end of this 3-through-7 age range, when peer influence begins. For the 8-through-12-year-old, by contrast, a sneaker's design details are carefully observed—from color to graphic design to the brand logo design and other features. Brand loyalty also emerges significantly during this 8-through-12 stage of development, not only because of these neurological and cognitive advances, but because of increased social sensitivities to what's "in" and what's "cool."

CONSUMABLES: Given increased ability to judge, evaluate, and distinguish, preadolescents will begin to be much more discriminating when it comes to the foods and beverages they prefer. In the previous stage, Mom typically was primarily in charge of which foods and beverages to purchase and put in front of her children. Not so with the 8-through-12-year-old. First of all, she has more independence and pocket money to spend. This translates to more purchase and consumption away from home, such as at fast-food establishments and convenience marts. Secondly, this older child becomes much more influential and involved in restaurant choices and with what gets written down on Mom's shopping list.

TECHNOLOGY: Whether it's electronic games, computer games, computer software, CD players, stereos, or sophisticated TV sets, the preteen is definitely primed for involvement with technology because his newly developing cognitive ability allows for the increased complexity that this technology demands. Unlike an adult, who is pulled apart and distracted by the many demands of his responsibilities and interests, the 8-through-12-year-old is not so distracted; his more focused orientation to time provides him the luxury of hours free to concentrate on technology.

PERCEPTION

The following filter model illustrates the "perceptual window" through which the 8-to-12-year-old looks at the world.

FIGURE 6.1: A MODEL OF THE INFORMATION-PROCESSING FILTER OF THE 8-THROUGH-12-YEAR-OLD

IMPLICATIONS

The Swiss psychologist Jean Piaget is the pioneer of research and analysis in this area of children's perception. Through his experiments he clearly distinguished the evolution of a child's perception through its developing years. As children transition into this preadolescent stage, they have in place most all the thinking and perceptual tools of an adult. The only significant skill yet to develop is the ability to do advanced abstract thinking, which evolves toward the end of this period—the kind of cognitive ability that is required, for example, by algebra or geometry. This advanced ability to think abstractly is also paralleled by the extremely important metacognitive skill of self-reflection—the ability to observe and think about one's own thoughts.[4]

With the preteen's developing logical abilities comes attention to and appreciation of details. The decor of a child's room *before* this stage of development—for example, a room's wallpaper, curtains, bedspreads, pictures and wall hangings—whether the room is themed around Barney or *Winnie the Pooh* or has ruffles and lace or sports icons is relatively unnoticed. As children advance into the 8-through-12 stage, however, these details start to be perceived as important and as an expression of one's emerging self. As children enter this older stage of development, room decor that is perceived as "too infantile" or "not cool" is "out"; room decor that reflects the 8-through-12-year-old's interests and room accessories that are acceptable with friends are "in."

How a preadolescent sees the world is determined by a whole host of factors, many of them social—what's "fun to do," what's "in" and "cool" and what "looks good" to his peers, and what's necessary to survive and thrive in school and at home. In Figure 6.1 above, the term "group-oriented" appears. The 8-through-12-year-old's window on the world includes an increasing concern for his peers and what they think, what they value, what they prefer—and what their opinions are about him.

This concern for the judgments and evaluations of others virtually drives and determines many of the tastes and preferences of this socially vulnerable 8-through-12-year-old, from what kinds of sneakers to wear to fast-food restaurant preferences to what sports are the coolest to participate in. Perceptually, one of the "filters" through which this preteen views the world is a "conformity filter." This peer awareness and sensitivity, or "peer pressure," becomes a significant force during this Rule/Role stage, in which this age child is driven to "fit in" and be liked.

NEEDS

Children at any age need love, safety, growth, and other basic needs such as food and shelter. And certainly their need for stimulation and fun play activities remains strong throughout this period. Important to look at in this "needs" area are the two needs that are particularly important to and germane to this 8-through-12 developmental stage.

A. ACCEPTANCE: The preteen's need for acceptance is essentially the need to feel OK and approved of by the important people in his life: his parents, his siblings, and his peers. This need is particularly strong during this formational period because of an expanded cognitive awareness and the social sensitivities that come with that awareness. The 8-through-12-year-old's view of himself, including his self-esteem, is taking form during this sensitive period; he is deciding many things about himself, such as "Am I attractive?" "Am I smart?" "Do people like me?—Am I popular?" Most all of this decision-making goes on unconsciously and is imperceptible to the eyes and ears of others, such as parents and teachers. Often outside appearances are very deceiving; a quite attractive child may conclude that he is ugly and a bright child may delude herself into believing she is relatively average or even stupid. During this period communication with caring adults is essential to "surface" many of these formational conclusions about the child's identity so that they can be brought to awareness and dealt with.

B. SUCCESS: As children evolve into this preteen age range, for the first time they start to concern themselves, consciously or unconsciously, with what it might take to survive on their own and succeed in the real world. And they now have the cognitive abilities to sort this out for themselves. The net effect is that the need to succeed drives them toward attempting to answer key questions for themselves: What are the rules and how can I deal with them? What's good/bad, right/wrong? What roles are out there in society and which of them do I want to emulate? Much of the learning that takes place during this period is through experience and the emulation of role models in real life and via entertainment and sports.

IMPLICATIONS

If I am, for example, a game developer or a software developer or if I'm concerned with package design on a child-targeted beverage or the use of the company's logo on apparel, I can appeal to a child in this age group based on my understanding of his particular needs—for example, his needs for acceptance and success. If I were a sneaker manufacturer, for example, I would take care to utilize graphic designs, colors, and logos that will be perceived to be "cool" by this age group and I would avoid approaches that would be seen as "for younger kids," "geeky," or otherwise "uncool." If I were a board game developer with 8-through-12-year-old girls as my target, I would take care to portray real-life kids on my packaging and use board game designs that would be perceived as "old enough" and "cool" rather than "too young," outdated, or otherwise not "cool." If I am conscious of these needs of my target it will greatly increase the likely attractiveness of my product to this more socially sensitive age group.

COOPERATION: These 8-through-12-year-olds much more often play in pairs and groups, unlike younger children, who spend more time playing alone. This has important ramifications for product and program development. Do I design games that emphasize solo play or team play? Do I present characters on my packaging that are solo or that are represented in a dynamic relationship with each other? The point to remember is that relationships between people become very important during this stage. Packaging and advertising that shows kids interacting with each other and the product are typically preferred over approaches that lack these elements.

COMPETITION: This is also a time for stronger competition. Engaging in competition with others is the primary means by which a child this age figures out what he's good at and what he's not good at and where he stands relative to others. More for males than for females, competition in sports and games (electronic, board, card, schoolyard, neighborhood) is particularly attractive at this stage of development. The success of certain apparel companies, such as Nike with its "Just Do It" campaign and its use of emulatory sports heroes and, to cite another case, a line of apparel designed around a "No Fear" message make perfect sense, given what's up with the 8-through-12-year-old.

THE MORAL SENSE

The 8-through-12-year-old is beginning to develop a more sophisticated moral sense. Younger kids are characterized by "black-and-white thinking"—that is, things are either right or wrong, good or bad (without an ability to perceive or understand much gray in between), and things are good/bad, right/wrong because someone in authority has said so. With the advent of greatly increased reasoning power made possible by the development of the left hemisphere of the cortex, children aged 8 through 12 begin to see moral issues in a whole new way; they don't accept others' points of view carte blanche but instead begin to question authority.

Not that this age group is out to overthrow conventional thinking. (A segment of the next stage, the adolescent stage of development is up to this, however.) Quite the contrary, kids this age are primarily trying to fit in. Moral questioning gives them the opportunity to uncover for themselves the rules that make the social world work. Their goal is primarily conformity. Thus the term "conventional morality" is used to describe this age child's stage of moral development. (For those of you who are parents of rebellious, free-thinking 10-year-olds, they are more the exceptions to the rule—if it's any consolation. You either have a problem on your hands, or an eccentric, or a genius—or all the above.)

IMPLICATIONS

It's no accident that around corporate board rooms and meeting rooms of companies that are targeting the preadolescent, the focus is more often than not on "what's in" and "what's out" and "what's cool" for this age child. Right or wrong, the 8-through-12-year-old is quite malleable and open to influence. He doesn't yet have the ego strength or self-sense to "think for himself" very effectively. Sensitivity to this fact is important. Developers should take great care with any moral implications communicated via their product, program, and advertising content. The 8-through-12-year-old is also hungry to identify with and emulate "heroes," e.g., in sports and the media. Sensitivity to this need as well is encouraged on the part of these important societal personalities and the companies that use them to get their messages across.

SELF/SOCIAL DEVELOPMENT

The preteen is essentially a conformist and quite group-oriented in the sense that he looks outside himself for what to believe and how to behave. Not yet into the teen years when he may begin to break away from the conventions of his parents, his church, and his school, the 8-through-12-year-old is busy "fitting in." As stated earlier, this is also an important formative period for this child's self-esteem, and many conclusions about his abilities, his looks, his strengths and weaknesses, and his overall worth are being arrived at during these years.

IMPLICATIONS

This is a time for belonging. Group activities such as clubs, teams, or organizations such as Fox Kids Club, Boy Scouts and Girl Scouts, AYSO soccer, church groups, etc., are very attractive to this age child, given a need to fit in and belong.

The 8-through-12-year period is also an egotistical age (in a natural sense; this no way implies a negative) in that he is very attracted to things that are personalized, things that give him a sense of self-importance and self-worth. Anything personal and self-customized will be attractive, therefore. Personal magazine subscriptions, meaningful logos from sports teams, heroic icons—all these are on target for this cohort.

THE "BILLBOARD EFFECT": This age child's increased sensitivities to the thoughts, opinions, judgments, and evaluations of others lead to something we refer to as the "Billboard Effect": 8-through-12-

year-olds as a rule become quite sensitive to what can be worn out in public or what might be known about them that could be ridiculed. While a 10-year-old girl, for example, may still play with dolls in her room or still love to sleep on her Winnie the Pooh sheets, she typically wouldn't dare wear a Winnie the Pooh blouse out in public—like a billboard—unless it were considered to be "cool" by her peers. An 11-year-old boy may still like to watch *Muppet Babies* cartoons in the safety of his own home, but he wouldn't be caught dead wearing a Muppet Babies sweatshirt to school.

HUMOR

In the previous 3-through-7 stage of development, humor that was too abstract, such as puns, sarcasm, or innuendo, could not be comprehended. Now, in the 8-through-12 stage, due to the development of the left-hemisphere processing skills that allow for comprehension of simple abstractions, the ability to understand more abstract humor is fast developing.

DARK-SIDE APPEAL

Of particular note is the great attraction that the preteen (again, males more than females) feels for the darker side of life. Whether it be horror stories, violent action games, movies or TV shows, or increased interest in the gross, the irreverent, and the taboo, these darker aspects of life become quite involving. Much of this content, like the grossness of snot and boogers and scatological and flatulent emissions, is funny *because* it's taboo. In fact, it is our view that the fact that this age child is busy attempting to find out what the rules are and what's good and bad (he's busy developmentally trying to be a "good boy") may unconsciously increase his attraction to these "bad-boy" elements in society. The dark-side and irreverent actions of certain cartoon characters, such as Ren and Stimpy and Garfield, for example, or the latest bad-boy antics of a rebellious sports hero may result in increased attraction because of this underground dark-side appeal.

It's also important to keep in mind, though, that simpler forms of humor such as slapstick, pie-in-the-face, *Home Alone,* Road Runner, Tasmanian Devil, Jim Carrey types of humor remain very appropriate and involving for the preadolescent.

IMPLICATIONS

The implications of humor for the preteen should be clear from the above discussion. Humor that is slapstick or mildly gross, violent, or irreverent is most often the form of humor that attracts and involves. It's important to add that this age child is not yet very sophisticated in the ways of the world and has not yet really become sexual. Forms of humor that deal with such things as political issues, ethnicity, or sexuality typically "go over his head."

SUMMARY

Again, we'll use the YMS Product Leverage Matrix—Figure 6.2—to briefly highlight the six most pertinent aspects of the Matrix as they relate to the 8-through-12-year-old.

CONCEPT: Whereas before this stage of development concepts needed to be of a simpler, less abstract variety, now concepts can be more complicated and more abstract. There are of course hundreds of concepts from many different categories that target the 8-through-12-year-old. Let's look at a few categories:

Games: Whereas simpler, unidimensional board games, card games, and electronic games were the order of the day for the below-8 set, now, given the 8-through-12-year-old's increased cognitive abilities, far more complicated and challenging games are demanded. Sophisticated board games such as Chess and Monopoly work well for this age, and electronic games are ideal, given their complexity, variety, and challenge.

Toys: There is in most cases a dramatic shift in the types of toys played with by the 8-through-12-year-old. In fact, most objects labeled "toys" are considered to be "for little kids" and "for younger than me" by this age child. Whatever the label, play activities for the preteen still exist even though they have changed. How have they changed? Certain toys such as Barbie® or GIJoe can sustain interest for a while because of their "reality" context (Barbie is a real girl; GIJoe figures are modeled after real military characters) and because they offer collectible detail. Electronic games, much to the chagrin of the toy industry, have come to replace a good deal of traditional toy play for a great many boys but fewer girls. A conservative estimate is that approximately 20

FIGURE 6.2: THE PRODUCT LEVERAGE MATRIX

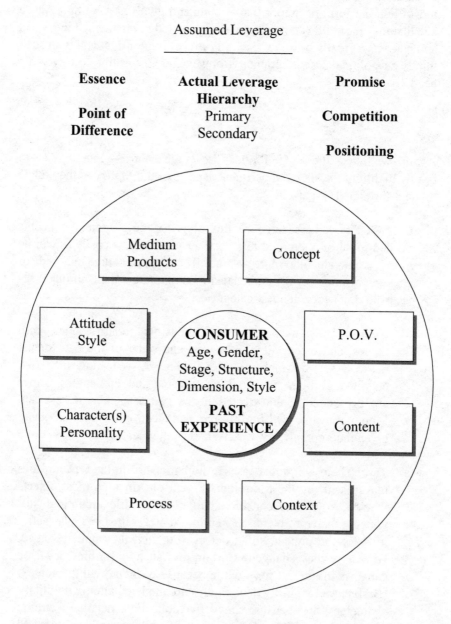

© 1997 YMS Consulting/Innertainment Inc.

percent of electronic game play is by girls. This does not mean, however, that this 20 percent of girls are all *purchasing* the games. A common scenario is that many girls are playing their brothers' or their friends' games.

The use of sports toys (balls, bats, gloves, rollerblades, bikes, rackets, etc.) also increases at this age, given the increased level of 8-through-12-year-olds participating in sports.

The toy industry has pulled a lot of doll hair out over how to reach this elusive 8-through-12-year-old more effectively. The bottom line is that these kids don't frequent traditional toy stores nearly as much as before. The toy companies that are going to succeed are those that recognize that they're not just in the toy business, they're in the play activity business, and this implies a reorientation toward products and programs that coincide with the preteen's expanding interests and lifestyle.

Foods and Beverages: Because the "billboard effect" doesn't have as much effect inside the safety of one's own home, food and beverage producers (whose products are consumed at home) can get away with using "younger" images and characters in their packaging and advertising. A Trix Rabbit, therefore, can continue to sustain a good deal of appeal for this age group. In like fashion, so can using the Animaniacs on Life cereal or Tasmanian Devil for a juice-drink campaign. "Heroic" or comedic icons such as Batman or Jim Carrey can also be used to advantage by this industry.

PROCESS: "Process" refers to such things as the slow, medium, or fast pacing of visual/auditory mediums such as advertising, TV, and film. The 8-through-12-year-old's increased cognitive abilities bring with them not only an acceptance of faster pacing, but an actual demand for it. MTV is pointed to as the innovator of a quick-cut, fast-paced approach to visual and auditory entertainment, and this "process" innovation has transformed the ways in which age 8+ individuals interact with a variety of media.

"Process" also refers to the "processing of information." As indicated in his book, *Playing the Future,* subtitled *"How Kids' Culture Can Teach Us to Thrive in an Age of Chaos,"* Douglas Rushkoff underlines how processes are changing, due in great part to technology.[5] Compare, for example, how people traditionally watched TV before the advent of the remote-control device. Typically we would watch whole programs, sometimes sticking to the same channel/network for the entire evening. Now, with the remote and screens within screens, we are more likely to be tuning in and out on a variety of programs every half hour. This more fragmented and chaotic world is the world in which today's children are growing up. Their relationship to speed and sequence and logic, for example, is dramatically different from previous generations'. The jury is out on whether this alteration in the processes that surround our young people (and all of us) is resulting in negative or positive effects on us as human beings, or may be some combination of the two. We must be vigilant to discern those effects and their impact on ourselves and our children.

CHARACTERS: Characters that would be perceived by a preadolescent as being childish or babyish are definitely not viewed as "cool" anymore. So it's a natural and healthy transition for an 8-through-12-year-old to move away from these simpler characters such as Barney or *Sesame Street* characters or Tweety Bird. (Nostalgically, however, some of these characters may survive in a preteen's room as part of their life, e.g., in stuffed-animal form as part of a "collection" atop an 11-year-old girl's bed.) Cartoon characters that score big in their appeal to the 8-through-12-year-old are typically those with more dark-side qualities such as sarcasm, ridicule, threat, soft violence, and irreverence: Bugs Bunny, Ren and Stimpy, the Animaniacs, Garfield, and the Rugrats. Comic-book characters with their more complex, more sophisticated and darker images, also thrive.

Notably, real-life character/heroes also are very appealing at this age: movie stars, action heroes, sports heroes. It's refreshing to note that in surveys of 8-through-12-year-olds, when they were asked who was their hero, the biggest vote-getter was someone quite real: "my Dad."

Given the increased cognitive sophistication of this age child as well as his/her social agenda of learning how to interrelate with others, there is also an increased interest that emerges during this time in the relationships and dynamics between characters.

ATTITUDE AND P.O.V.: "Attitude" and "P.O.V." or "Point of View" refer to whether a product or program is conservative, nonconservative, or somewhere in between. As suggested by references above to dark-side appeal and the power of the gross, the violent, and the irreverent and taboo regarding both this age group and later ones, there is a lot more latitude for product and programming that is edgier and more controversial—as long as it doesn't "step over the line." And that "line" appears to be stretching toward more and more liberalism all the time.

CONTEXT: As has been touched on before, the 3-through-7-year-old, with his less-developed logical abilities and limited experience, does not relate effectively to either the past or the future; he is very "now" oriented. With the development of the left hemisphere, however, past and future are more understandable and easier to relate to. Programs about dinosaurs or sci-fi space, therefore, are very appropriate for this older child.

Context also refers to geographical setting. The 8-through-12-year-old is expanding his knowledge of and appreciation for different places and peoples, so the Earth and indeed the entire solar system are now fair game.

MEDIUM/PRODUCTS: Whereas toys, simple games, books, ride-ons, bicycles, and cartoon shows were some of the emphasized "mediums" for targeting 3-through-7-year-olds, there is an expanded variety of mediums with which to target 8-through-12-year-olds. After all, these preteens are fast becoming adult-like and independent, and are potential purchasers in a broad variety of categories: computers, clothing, music, fast food, beverages, snacks, games, magazines, personal hygiene items, etc. Their *influence* over family purchasing is also on the rise—from the brand of toothpaste or computer to buy to the make and model of the family car.

ON TO ADOLESCENCE

If there is such a phenomenon as the "terrible twos" there most certainly is the phenomenon of the "treacherous teens." As we shift gears from the relatively passive and innocent calm waters of the preteen and younger child and move into the stormy waters of adolescence, a whole host of changes take place, not least among them—puberty.

CHAPTER 7

AGES 13 THROUGH 15
Early Adolescence

> Don't laugh at a youth for his affections; he is only trying
> on one face after another to find a face of his own.
> —Logan Smith, *Afterthoughts*[1]

E arly adolescence brings with it significant changes. First, puberty hits hard and fast with all its accompanying biochemical and hormonal changes. These physiological changes dramatically affect the related psychological drives, moods, and behaviors of the adolescent. (There is also, by the way, recent information indicating that the onset of puberty is occurring at an earlier age.)

Second, this developmental stage reflects the first major opening to abstract thinking. In what is often called the period of formal operations, this age youth can now operate in abstractions, and can, assuming his brain has sufficiently developed, engage in full metacognitive functions, that is, think about his own thinking. These neural and cognitive developments alter humor and creativity, providing access to new and previously unexplored territory. This age child, for example, can now begin to creatively challenge established belief systems and points of view, and can understand the subtleties of innuendo, sarcasm, and irony.

Early adolescence is also the key period of identity formation, when the adolescent is pushed to establish his own niche or point of view, which often is in direct conflict with his/her elders and the establishment. This push often results in unusual mood swings and distancing from parents and more conventional "others" such as teachers. Looking good, power, self-esteem, dating, and social acceptance are critical to the early adolescent. This adolescent may believe that he is fully mature in spite of his lack of knowledge and experience. It is a time when peers play an enormous role in decision making, even overshadowing many parents.

It is also a period of experimentation; interest in sex, drugs, and rock and roll on the part of many young teens is symptomatic of the teen's push toward the formation of his identity as separate from established points of view. It is a period of postconventional morality made possible in particular by evolving cognitive abilities, a period in which our budding teen is often looking beyond what he has been told up to this point and starting to think for himself.

The typical early adolescent also begins to seek out support from and affiliation with a social subgroup or clique such as the campus athletes, school leaders, rebels, nerds, or outcasts. He will gravitate toward the type of group that satisfies his/her needs for acceptance, self-esteem, and personal power. Typically his choice will be based on matching his own emerging sense of himself, his abilities and interests, with those of the individuals he chooses to affiliate with.

The 13-through-15-year-old's entertainment choices may, therefore, directly reflect his need to "fit in" with his newly chosen social group. Underlying these needs in many of these adolescent groups is an attraction to bizarre, dark-side, and often socially unacceptable forms of entertainment as a way to break away from more conservative points of view that brand these darker expressions as taboo. This dark-side appeal is rooted in a number of adolescent needs. First, it is important that the adolescent establish his own separate identity, distinct from established family and social values. Next, there is a natural "push" for the adolescent to reject the status quo in favor of something "farther out," new and antiestablishment. This push is coupled, in many cases, with a newly acquired idealism, which stems from blossoming intellectual skills related to significant changes in brain development. This idealism can be both refreshing and trying as teens question current thinking and values.

It's important to note that not all adolescents fit the mold of "rebellious teenagers." While this need to establish oneself as distinct from one's parents is present to some degree in all teens, many do not manifest any overt signs of separation; in fact many identify strongly with the views and ways of being of their parents, teachers, and church leaders, remaining quite conservative throughout adolescence.

All children, and the early adolescent for certain, are learning to process visual and auditory stimuli faster and more efficiently and are demanding higher and higher levels of information to keep their attention. Currently, technology, the media, and advertising are inventing new and more compressed visual and auditory images and stimuli displays, partially because of economics and partially because of digitalization. MTV and video gaming have contributed an entirely different way to process information through "sight bites" and "sound bites," and today's young people have learned to expect this high-paced stimulation from the media. The entertainment media appear to be constantly altering the nature of information to satisfy the perceptual appetites of the young.

INCREASED INDEPENDENCE

The beginning of the adolescent years also marks the advent of increased independence. Early teens go unsupervised to the movies or malls more often, shop on their own more frequently, and certainly make their own decisions about item and brand purchases much more independently than ever before.

In a section on "The Young Consumer," for example, the 1996 *Roper Youth Report* (see Table 7.1) lists the product categories below and asks 6-through-17-year-olds their level of purchase decision-making without parental influence. Beginning at age 13 the shift toward much more independent purchasing can readily be seen.

WINNERS

What "wins" with the 13-through-15-year-old is, in many cases, dramatically different than for younger age segments. Whereas the Barneys and Barbie® dolls and Power Rangers of the world—or the next "hit" that comes along—appear to be able to capture large segments of their respective age segments, this early teen appears to be more selective in what interests her. To focus on apparel, for example, those items and brands that have captured the most awareness and acceptance among her peers definitely have a "leg up" on competing offerings—e.g., Nike, Guess!, the Levi's of the world. This phenomenon of brand consciousness increases during the teen years as a direct result of increasing peer influence and increased abilities of discernment.

Early teens are also very activity oriented—especially as they begin to leave the "nest" more frequently and venture out into the world with their peers. And if activity orientation is the key, then we need only ascertain which activities are the most popular for the 13-through-15-year-old to determine which categories of product or program could vie for "winner status." According to the Roper Youth Report and other sources, the activities listed at the top of page 110 rank high with this age group.

Table 7.1: Items Chosen for Purchase Without Consulting Parents

16. Here is a list of products. Please read down the list and for each one tell me if it is something you *usually* pick out for yourself without needing to ask a parent about before choosing, or is it something you usually need to check with a parent before choosing, or if it is something your parent chooses for you, or do you never buy it?

| | **1996** | | | | | | |
| | **6–17** | **6–7** | | **8–12** | | **13–17** | |
	Total %	**Boys %**	**Girls %**	**Boys %**	**Girls %**	**Boys %**	**Girls %**
Candy or snacks	74	36	39	73	63	94	94
Soft drinks	73	36	28	73	69	92	90
Food from fast food places	66	31	37	61	53	87	89
Books	56	19	30	50	50	68	82
Games or toys	53	19	29	50	39	76	69
Clothes	48	NA	NA	30	23	71	70
Athletic shoes or sneakers	47	NA	NA	28	25	68	69
Compact disc or tapes	46	4	9	34	26	75	81
Magazines	45	11	12	32	29	70	79
Jewelry	38	NA	NA	14	31	40	70
Video games	36	13	11	33	17	66	49
Video movie rentals	36	11	14	24	16	64	60
Personal care products	32	NA	NA	11	15	45	59
Video movies you buy	32	NA	NA	16	10	53	49
Computer software/ CD-ROMs	12	1	—	7	3	25	20

Note: "NA" denotes item not asked of 6–7-year-olds; (—) denotes no mentions.
1996 *Roper Youth Report.* Copyright © 1996 Roper Starch Worldwide, Inc., 205 East 42nd Street, New York, NY 10017.

Organized sports	Team sports such as baseball, basketball, volleyball
Independent sports	Rollerblading, skateboarding, swimming
Electronic games	Dedicated systems (such as Nintendo, Sega, and Sony) and computer games
Computers	Nongame use, e.g., for school work and Internet activity
Television viewing	Especially sitcoms and sophisticated cartoons such as *The Simpsons,* action/drama like *ER*
Movies	Both in-theater and home video
Shopping	Especially for key items of interest, such as food and beverage, personal hygiene, apparel, and recreational/fun items such as games and sports items
School activities	Clubs, music, band, drama, sports, and social events
Church or synagogue activities	Choir, prayer groups, scripture study groups, volunteer work, social groups
Reading	Less books and more magazines and newspapers

It's important to note that there is also a substantial increase in activities with friends over previous years. Teens are very social creatures and tend to gravitate toward friends and social-group activities far more than previous age segments. What they are seeking in this migration is the establishment of their own unique identities in relationship to and against the backdrop of parent and family identities.

TARGETING TEENS

Many child- and youth-targeting companies have been very frustrated in their attempts to reach the "tween" and the early and late adolescent with their products and programs. While certain categories such as electronic games and apparel are "layered" in such a way that they offer significant payoff or benefit to preteens as well as teens, many categories such as toys (not sports toys), and child-targeted foods and beverages are limited to preteen interest.

The teen is rapidly moving toward adult tastes and choices and is increasingly tending toward preferring adult-marketed items—just to cite one example, adult-packaged frozen foods rather than younger-targeted items with cartoon characters on them. The implication of this is twofold. First, know your limitations. Perhaps you should expend your efforts on increasing your effectiveness with younger targets rather than pursuing teen targets. Second, look for ways to custom design your product for teen tastes and interests, perhaps even linking your product or program to already established activities and interests engaged in by the 13-through-15 target.

BRAND LOYALTY: The issues of brand awareness, brand identification, and brand loyalty are important to consider for the developing youth. In certain categories, such as toys and games and TV programming, brand makes little difference; what matters is what product or program delivers the greatest play or entertainment value. At the same time, however, other categories lend themselves to early brand identification and loyalty, especially beginning approximately at the teen years—categories such as personal hygiene (many adult women use the same brand of lipstick that they used as teens), computers, apparel, and even automobiles. At YMS we have often marveled at the fact that more adult-targeting companies, such as automobile companies, gasoline companies, and beverage companies, don't address these early brand identification patterns by targeting younger audiences.

In order to understand the underlying dynamics of the early teen and therefore what drives his interests and motivations, let's look at the core elements that differentiate this developmental stage from previous stages.

Common Denominators for Success	
Neurological	M-System: Midbrain or Limbic system is ideally fully developed and in place by about age 11 C-System: Right hemisphere of cortex (4–15) Left hemisphere of cortex (7+)
Cognitive	Formal operations, logic, abstraction
Needs	Independence, acceptance, sexuality, early identity, self-esteem, success
Moral sense	Conventional, Postconventional
Perception	Sight bites, sound bites, reality-based fantasy, high pacing, high sensual, high variability
Self/Social	Identity, independence from parents, sexuality, peer approval needs, relationships
Humor	Slapstick, dark-side, bizarre, abstract, word play, puns

In order to get at what implications each of these elements has for successful product development and marketing, let's explore them in detail.

NEUROLOGY AND COGNITION

Ideally, the midbrain's development is fully in place at about age 11—"ideally," because if there are significant deficiencies in a child's upbringing, notably if the mother–child emotional bonding is insufficient, or if there are such other deficiencies as nutritional inadequacies, the midbrain may be complete in its physical development but may be impaired in its abilities and capacities due to limited dendritic connections with the later-emerging frontal lobe. It is the midbrain that accounts for, among many other functions, the ability to imagine; this imaginative ability is critical for other left-hemisphere cognitive functions such as problem-solving, impulse control, and empathic response to the needs of others.

The most important neurological brain development, and therefore thinking development, occurs during this period with the evolution of the cognitive ability known as "formal operations." This means that the 13-through-15-year-old (given full brain and cognitive development to this point) is able to think more effectively beyond the simple "black or white" of things and now can see the "gray" in between. He can now also think about and handle problems with high levels of abstraction and complexity. He has the ability to take a problem apart (analysis), fully explore it from a variety of angles, and put a solution together (synthesis) as well as monitor what works and doesn't work (evaluation).

IMPLICATIONS

This age group is motivated to exercise its increasingly sophisticated cognitive abilities. This translates into higher interest and involvement in such activities as complex electronic games; more complex board and card games such as chess, poker, and bridge; and more sophisticated reading material such as newspapers.

Many of the trappings of earlier childhood will of necessity be shed. For example, toys that are unidimensional and not complex will fall away (partly under pressures from the early adolescent's peers that require him to eschew products and programs that might brand him as childish). Simple electronic games will be "beneath him" in that he has either mastered them or he finds them to be not complex or abstract enough. This age group will also lose interest in TV programming that is too simple and does not deliver sufficiently complex characters, content, and humor.

Characters such as Bugs Bunny and Garfield survive and thrive in the eyes of the 13+ year-olds in large part because of what we call "perceptual filters." If I am 5 years old I perceive Bugs as a funny bunny with a unique voice and I appreciate his slapstick pie-in-the-face humor, especially his manipulations and outsmartings of Elmer Fudd, his archnemesis. But most of the *verbal* humor—the sarcasm, puns, innuendo—goes right over my head. If I am 9 years old I see a conniving and funny rabbit; I still appreciate the slapstick humor but now I am also able to appreciate a good deal of the more sophisticated humor and sarcasm. By the time I am 13+ I am fully equipped neurologically and cognitively to understand just about all of Bugs's humor and still am greatly entertained by his slapstick antics.

By the age of approximately 14 all but one final brain/thinking development is in place—and that is the full development of the prefrontal lobe. It is this development that expands the child's ability to be empathic, to love unconditionally, and to fully be able to appreciate another person's perspective. (If you've ever had pre–15-year-olds and you've wondered about their seemingly extreme selfishness and seeming inability to appreciate your or another's point of view, you may be comforted to understand that this behavior is in part a function of the development of the evolving brain.)

PERCEPTION

Figure 7.1 illustrates the "perceptual window" through which the 13-through-15-year-old views his world.

FIGURE 7.1: A MODEL OF THE PERCEPTUAL FILTER OF THE 13-TO-15-YEAR-OLD

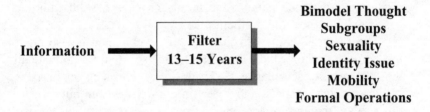

The world that the 13-through-15-year-old is now seeing is a more complex world than he saw in previous developmental stages. In addition to more advanced cognitive abilities, both his social needs and his hormones are pushing him toward a variety of changes. He now has to deal with his own identity formation. "Who am I?" "Who am I becoming?" Rather than blindly following certain role models, he now has an ability to discriminate (though we adults might not think so) more effectively between these icons. And as we shall see, this age child's needs are shifting him out of home-and-parent dependency and into increased independence and a peer dependency pattern or at least into a life of dual affiliations—many times fraught with conflict.

Perceptually, the early teen also responds to and demands more complex stimuli—both because he is now able cognitively to process it, and because of how media such as MTV and today's fast-paced commercials have conditioned him. He typically prefers, for example, TV and movies with faster pacing, quick sight and sound bites, and complex images.

NEEDS

In early adolescence the following needs come to the foreground and demand satisfaction:

> *Self-esteem needs,* particularly *love, acceptance,* and *success*
> *Identity*
> *Sexuality*

SELF-ESTEEM: If our 13-through-15-year-old is to experience high self-esteem he needs to satisfy his need for *love, acceptance,* and *success.* The need for parental love remains constant through these early adolescent years although it may appear to "go underground" due to pressing peer acceptance and identity issues. That is, this age child—while needing and wanting love from his parents—may not be able to socially afford to display this love or accept this love in public. Still, young teens need to believe that they are loved. Receiving this love as a constant from their parents and family provides a solid emotional base and helps them to love themselves.

The 13-through-15-year-old stage of development is also one of the periods during which our young adolescent most dramatically feels the need for acceptance. He needs this acceptance from his peers, his parents and teachers, and—very importantly—from himself. It is this strong drive toward acceptance from his peers as well as his drive to establish his own identity separate from his parents that often propels the early adolescent toward "desirable" or "undesirable" subgroups, today's equivalents of the "Cheerleaders," the "Jocks," the "Nerds," or "Techies" with the double rings of keys at their belts, the "Loadies," the "Rock 'n' Rollers," or the "Gangbangers."

While in many cases his need for acceptance may predominate, the 13-through-15-year-old also experiences the need to succeed—although not as deeply or urgently as when he enters the late adolescent stage (16+) and experiences the reality of having to survive on his own. At the same time, for some early teens, a counterforce against success may be the subgroup that he identifies with, as he will invariably take on the values of his subgroup. If his subgroup's values run contrary to conventional notions of success, succeeding in school and other "society-approved" markers of success may fall by the wayside.

IDENTITY: This early adolescent begins to deal with the questions "Who am I?" and "Who am I becoming?" In his dealing with these ego-forming issues, he may appear to be struggling, or "breezing through," or somewhere in between, depending on his own particular journey and the circumstances, blessings, and obstacles that present themselves during this period. What many parents fail to understand is that one way or another their *teenage children need to establish their own identities* and in a large percentage of cases the form this takes is via separation from the values and attitudes of their parents—thus that feared phenomenon called "Rebellion." In these cases there is no such thing as "rebel without a cause," as the cause is rebellion itself, in order to establish the teenager's sense of self as separate and distinct from his parents and other conventional authority figures. If during the teen years our children *do not* establish a strong sense of identity— either through rebellion or adoption of conventional values or some mix of the two—then they may reach adulthood overly codependent.

SEXUALITY: A third "need" that surfaces and demands to be dealt with during the teen years is the teen's sexuality. This is a complex scenario that includes physiological changes; increased sexual awareness and interest; peer, parental, and religious attitudes and behaviors; and morality. How this drive to explore one's sexuality and evolve as a sexual being manifests varies greatly from individual to individual. For many young teens this drive develops but appears to remain relatively latent until years later, whereas for others it manifests quite radically, leading to sexual experimentation. The 1996 Roper Youth Report indicates that 35 percent of 13-through-17-year-olds indicate that sexual activity is a concern or problem for them.

IMPLICATIONS

What implications for product and program development and marketing can be drawn from the fact that 13-through-15-year-olds are dealing with the above needs for self-esteem (love, acceptance, and success), identity, and sexuality? The implications are many.

In many ways, the early teen period is a time of transition. In terms of product and program development and marketing the implication is profound. If I as a 13-through-15-year-old am moving away from myself as a child, I necessarily am also moving away from the things of childhood— my childhood "toys," games, apparel, and many of my childhood activities and interests. This "move away" is accented even more forcefully during the late adolescent stage but begins powerfully during the early teen years.

In addition, there is the "billboard effect." As discussed in the previous chapter on the 8-through-12-year-old, there are definite repercussions from one's peers if a 13-through-15-year-old wears or professes interest in or otherwise affiliates himself publicly (like a billboard) with products, programs, characters, or other concepts that are considered to be childish or beneath him. In the relative safety of his own home, however, he will have no trouble continuing to involve himself with some of those childish icons, products, and programs, such as enjoying the Trix Rabbit on his cereal box, or watching *Road Runner* cartoons.

Anything directly reflective of himself, however, such as his room decor, will likely change to coincide with his emerging identity. In our young teen male's room, down come the Power Rangers posters if they weren't already removed during the 8-through-12 stage, and even perhaps the X-Men, and up go the music group posters. In his female counterpart's room, down come the frou-frou curtains, and the dolls and stuffed animals may end up in storage as she transforms her room to fit her emerging identity. (Many girls, however, tend to remain attached to younger, "nostalgic" objects longer, and it is not surprising to walk into an early teen girl's room and have it still filled with childish icons and objects: Barbie displays, stuffed animal collections, *Winnie the Pooh* decor.) She would not, however, likely "billboard" these socially dangerous elements out in public.

Another implication of the early teen's emerging identity is the *increased independence* that comes along with it. Research clearly shows that children increasingly have more personal money to spend, and make more independent purchases, the older they get.

TEENS ARE ADULT-BOUND

To the chagrin of many child marketers who wish that he and she would stay interested in their younger products and programs, the teen is moving rapidly toward adult products and programs, e.g., in the foods and beverages area, the personal-hygiene and apparel categories—with a few notable exceptions, such as the types of entertainment they seek out. Early adolescent entertainment preferences for the most part differ both from more childish preferences and more mature adult preferences. The types of TV shows, music, and movies that teens and young adults tend to prefer are filled with more adolescent and young adult characters, icons, lyrics, and story lines. TV sitcoms (*Family Matters, Fresh Prince of Bel Air, Full House*) and dramas (*Beverly Hills 90210*) that have adolescent and young adult stars, stories, and humor, for example, are hugely popular among early and late adolescents. Shows such as *The Simpsons,* a prime-time cartoon show, remain popular also due to their edgy humor and content, which in some ways parallel the issues that young teens are dealing with.

THE MORAL SENSE

Armed with his near-complete neurology, the 13-through-15-year-old is now cognitively capable of going beyond polarized, black-and-white thinking and now can "see the gray" in between. This ability, along with more advanced critical thinking skills, allows this young adolescent the luxury of thinking for himself and actually going against the grain of conventional morality. More often than not, however, he will stumble a great deal along this new territorial path as he tries on one set of rights and wrongs and then the next—often ending up identifying with the morals of the subgroup he has affiliated himself with. This age child also finds himself transitioning from striving to adhere more strictly to the rules and roles of his parents and significant other authority figures toward more independent thinking. Unlike the 16-through-19-year-old who has ideally evolved to a point of solid "postconventional" moral thinking, this early adolescent is caught somewhere in between trying to sort out what's right/wrong and good/bad and just whom to identify with.

IMPLICATIONS

The task of product and program developers and marketers can become both more difficult and more simple due to what's occurring in the teen years. It can become more difficult if developers and marketers attempt to put all 13-through-15-year-olds in the same bag, and easier if they recognize the fragmentation that is happening in "teen society," and target subgroups effectively.

At the same time, however, there *are* some common threads. For example, TV sitcoms and dramas that deal with teen and young-adult issues of relationships, ethics, and "making it" in the world are targeting right to the bull's-eye of what adolescents are dealing with. The music industry needs to be more subgroup-targeted, however, in that musical preferences are primarily a result of three elements: (a) the music itself—beat, melody, musical genre, (b) the performers as icons and role models, and (c) the content of lyrics as a direct reflection of the subgroup's needs, wants, and values.

SELF/SOCIAL DEVELOPMENT

A development of great significance for the newly emerging adolescent is what might be termed *identity reformulation*. This stage of adolescence is in large part devoted to the question "Who am I?"—as a unique individual in the family and social matrix. This most challenging task of breaking

away from or at least examining conventional expectations in order to figure out who one is and what one's place is in society is a natural transition
for some and a drama-filled struggle for others.

Some parents are blessed with relatively smooth sailing during these
early adolescent years as their teens seem to glide through without much
turmoil. For other parents there are some rough waters but no hurricanes.
For still others it is a nightmare. How often have we heard the complaint of
a tormented early-teen parent: "It seems like just a month or two ago, she
was this wonderful, well-groomed, fully in communication, excited-to-be-
alive daughter of mine. Now I don't know who she is. She's disheveled,
brooding, irresponsible, has gotten a tattoo of a rattlesnake on her hip, and
hangs out with weird types the devil himself wouldn't be caught dead with.
Worst of all, she won't talk to me!"

IMPLICATIONS

Given the splintering of the teen population into subgroups, and what is
going on with our young adolescents on a variety of self and social fronts,
it would be useful to take a brief look at the impact this identity reformulation has on various product and program categories:

TOYS: Except for the small segment of the 13-through-15-year-old
population that is still into expanding their GIJoe or Barbie® collections, childhood toys are pretty much in our young teen's past. A
notable exception is sports toys such as Frisbees, skateboards,
rollerblades, sports equipment, and sports accessories.

GAMES: Simple board and card games are "out"; more complicated
games such as chess, Monopoly, Scrabble, and poker are "in." Electronic games are still very much "in"—especially with males—and a
notable shift is starting to emerge toward more reality-based electronic
games such as sports games, and toward challenging role-play games.

Given the expanded role and importance of friends and peer
groups in the early adolescent's life, it is important to note that the
amount of time spent at individual play decreases, and conversely the
amount of time spent in activities and play with others increases
steadily, during the teen years.

MOVIES: Other than childish cartoon movies such as the *Power
Rangers* movie and sophisticated adult dramas, movies, both in theaters and as home rentals, are hugely popular among all teens. Especially attractive are action-adventure movies, such as *Star Wars,*

Batman, Arnold Schwarzenegger–type movies, and comedies of the Jim Carrey sort.

TELEVISION: Especially attractive to the early adolescent are sitcoms that provide humor as well as sitcoms and dramas that deal with adolescent and young-adult issues—shows such as *Fresh Prince of Bel Air, Home Improvement, Friends,* and *Beverly Hills 90210. America's Funniest Home Videos,* with its slapstick, fall-down, pie-in-the-face humor, is ideal for this age group. Early adolescents will also enjoy straightforward (not too complicated) adult action dramas such as *ER,* and reality-based shows such as *COPS* and *Emergency 911.*

MUSIC: While middle-of-the-road pop music may have the broadest appeal, e.g., the music of Mariah Carey, studies like the Roper Youth Report show that loyalties are spread relatively wide among a host of other performers and types of music. Among the most popular of these are Michael Jackson, Bone Thugs-N-Harmony, Boyz II Men, Madonna, and Alannis Morrisette. Perhaps more than any other medium, music reflects the splintering of the adolescent culture into different subgroups, each with differing tastes.

SOFTWARE: Assuming that electronic computer games were included in "Games" above, our 13-through-15-year-old is most likely to utilize nongame electronic software to assist him with schoolwork—encyclopedia data as resource, word-processing for reports and assignments, learning-assist programs such as foreign-language, typing, and math. Some communications software will also appeal, such as printshop-type ware that produces cards and posters, and correspondence-related software.

PUBLICATIONS: Tracking the types of publications that early adolescents subscribe to and enjoy is very revealing of the shifts that are occurring in this age group. For example, 8-through-12-year-olds read more comic books than 13-through-15-year-olds; comic-book readership among early teens drops off. Early adolescents read fewer publications, first of all. Secondly, when they do read, they appear to read more reality-based publications; newspaper readership increases substantially during the teen years. In the same vein our early adolescent is transitioning away from *Sports Illustrated for Kids* toward the adult *Sports Illustrated.* Early-teen girls for the most part are interested in both teen magazines and adult women-targeted magazines, which emphasize glamour and relationship issues.

PERSONAL HYGIENE: Other than grooming and hygiene items that are targeted directly at teen problems such as pimples, there is little differentiation between adult items and teen-specific items in the personal hygiene marketplace. Early teens tend to gravitate toward adult products in this area; there have been some notable failures in attempts to develop personal grooming and hygiene products narrowly targeted to teens. This is not to say that future efforts in this direction might not succeed, given a powerful product line-up with a potent marketing angle.

FOODS AND BEVERAGES: This is another category in which teens have, for the most part, migrated away from kid-positioned products and toward teen- and adult-positioned products. Exceptions to this rule can be found in the cereal and snack-food categories, where early adolescents are still attracted to cartoonish characters on cereal boxes and on snack foods—the Trix Rabbit, Tony the Tiger, and a host of licensed characters such as the X-Men, the Animaniacs, Garfield, and Bugs Bunny. The Billboard Effect will keep a good deal of this more "childish" attraction restricted to the safety of their homes, however.

FAST FOOD: Fast food, whether it's take-out or home-delivered pizza or time to hang out at the local McDonald's, Hardee's, Taco Bell or Burger King, is right in the bull's-eye of what appeals to the early (or late) teen.

APPAREL: The 13-through-15-year-old is very much influenced by what's "in" and what's "out" in terms of what she wears. Indicative of this is the fact that Nikes and Reeboks were named along with "playing sports" and a host of other activities and objects when asked "What's *'in'* at school?" in the 1996 Roper Youth Report. Kids want to "look good" and be approved of by their peers; therefore peer influence is strong in the "what to wear" category.

HUMOR

Interestingly, slapstick physical forms of humor remain appealing and involving—even later on, through adulthood. Vaudeville was an example of this adult appeal earlier in this century. And the popularity among adolescents and adults of the fall-down, baby-splats-his face-in-his-birthday-cake type of humor of *America's Funniest Home Videos* is also indicative of this slapstick appeal.

With the development of an essentially full-blown capacity to think abstractly, however, comes the ability to understand and appreciate more subtle forms of humor such as sarcasm, innuendo, and irony. The early adolescent, therefore, is a more sophisticated audience than he was during earlier developmental stages.

SUMMARY

Let's look at the YMS Product Leverage Matrix, Figure 7.2, to isolate the key aspects of the matrix as they relate to the 13-to-15-year-old.

MEDIUM/PRODUCTS: As 13-through-15-year-olds move out of their "childhood" years and into adolescence they naturally are leaving behind certain activity and play patterns. Certain "mediums" or categories such as conventional toys and simple games and foods and beverages targeted to younger consumer audiences will, therefore, go by the wayside.

CONCEPT AND CONTENT: Because we are dealing with an almost fully developed neurology and all the more sophisticated cognitive abilities that go with it, the Concept and Content will necessarily need to be more complex, sophisticated, and challenging. Simpler, more juvenile TV concepts such as the *Power Rangers,* for example, will be replaced in the 13-through-15-year-old's viewing preferences by more complex concepts such as *The Simpsons.*

POINT OF VIEW AND ATTITUDE/STYLE: Just as Concept and Content need become more complex and sophisticated for this early adolescent, the P.O.V. and Attitude/Style of concepts should also reflect an increase in abstraction and sophistication. For example, humor that is more edgy, leaning toward the taboo—i.e., sexual—is sought after; movies with increased amounts of "edge," dark-side, and violence are preferred (by males). Graphic designs on packaging need more complexity and "attitude," i.e., modern, abstract, futuristic designs.

CHARACTERS/PERSONALITIES: Movie and TV characters and personalities that appeal especially to the adolescent are less unidimensional and simple and more complex overall. And, while a few cartoon remnants from their preadolescent years remain of interest— especially those characters with definite "edge" such as Bugs Bunny, Ren and Stimpy, Tasmanian Devil, and Garfield, most characters with

FIGURE 7.2: THE PRODUCT LEVERAGE MATRIX

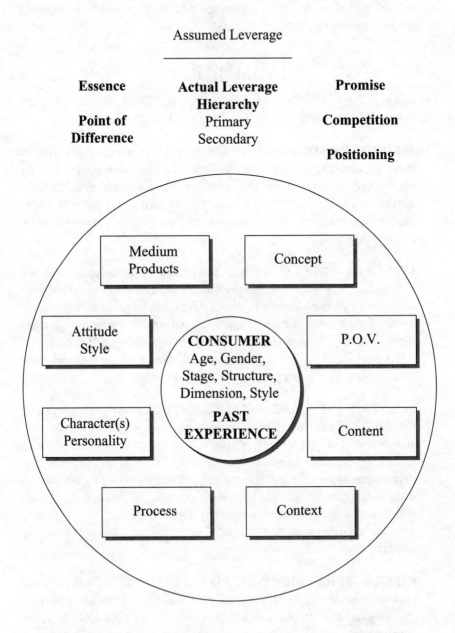

appeal to the 13-through-15-year-old are now more realistic rather than fantasy-based or idealistic. Star basketball player Michael Jordan, for example, is far and away the most popular personality/role model for the early adolescent, followed by Jim Carrey. It's no accident that Bugs Bunny and Michael Jordan have been teamed up together for TV commercials and movies, given their shared broad-based appeal to adolescents and young adults.

CONTEXT: Just as Content, Concept, and characters have become less fantasy-based, less unidimensional, and more realistic, so too does Context follow suit. Again, *Context*—the way we use the term at YMS Consulting—refers to time period and geographic locale. Given his increased cognitive skills, the early adolescent can deal with all sorts of time dimensions, including sci-fi and adventure time contexts—*Back to the Future, Star Wars, Braveheart.* He can also deal with more complex settings or locales, whether they appear in publications, electronic games on TV, in movies, or elsewhere.

PROCESS: "Process" refers to aspects of a concept such as pacing, visual, sound, and special effects, and editing techniques such as quick cuts, fast-paced images, multiple images, etc. By the time a child has reached adolescence, he has already been "conditioned"—to use a behavioral-psychology term—by MTV, TV advertising, and TV shows such as *NYPD Blue* to interact with and even prefer these more complicated and faster "process" elements.

THE END OF ADOLESCENCE

In the next chapter we move from early adolescence into the late adolescence of the 16-through-19-year-old. From the time of the "terrible twos" when tiny toddlers first learn to say "No!" to these last teen years, gaining autonomy so that one can live on one's own is the underlying task. This older teen is fast waking up to the fact that he is going to have to fend for himself and this "wake-up call" sets certain needs and behaviors in motion that were only stirring beneath the surface in the previous developmental stage.

CHAPTER 8

AGES 16 THROUGH 19

Late Adolescence

> The imagination of a boy is healthy, and the imagination
> of a mature man is healthy; but there is a space of life
> between in which the soul is in a ferment, the character
> undecided, the way of life uncertain, the ambition thick-
> sighted.
>
> John Keats, *Endymion*[1]

The late adolescent is quite a different creature from the early adolescent. There are essentially three factors that contribute to this difference: (a) The development of the prefrontal lobe, (b) completion of puberty, and (c) social mobility.

THE PREFRONTAL LOBE

Assuming neurological and emotional growth has proceeded normally up to this point, the last major brain development, what Joseph Chilton Pearce[2] calls the "entrainment" of the prefrontal lobe of the cortex, takes place during this period of late adolescence. By "entrainment" is meant that while other brain development proceeds at a normal pace, this prefrontal lobe area undergoes a more concentrated development during this period.

Research indicates that the complete and mature development of the prefrontal lobe is not a given. Lack of the emotional bonding that comes with parental love, lack of warm physical contact and emotional support, as well as emotional trauma or drug use can retard this development such that full prefrontal development does not occur. For example there is neurological research on violent criminals, such as the work of Adrian Raine at the University of Southern California.[3] Research into the prefrontal development of the brains of violent criminals in our prison system is beginning to indicate that a high percentage of them may not have fully integrated prefrontal lobes. This can translate to weak impulse control and lack of empathy—a fundamental lack of conscience, if you will. Unfortunately this lack appears to be irreversible. The "window of opportunity" for the full structural development of the prefrontal lobe of the brain appears to shut down after adolescence, and this "window" may never open again.

Research also indicates that the prefrontal lobe makes possible the highest and loftiest of mental and human functioning, sometimes referred to as the "executive function" of the brain: the ability to engage in metacognition or "thinking about one's own thinking," to empathize and to control impulse reaction. In addition, prefrontal development allows for increased problem-solving ability, increased ability to plan for the future, and a higher reflective capacity—in short, increased "space" between stimulus and response. Without this ability to pause and reflect and "put the brakes on" reactive emotional responses, a human being is in a sense emotionally and socially underdeveloped. He is "on rails" so to speak, a creature of automatic, reactive responses.

You're on the freeway and you accidentally cut someone off. He goes berserk, swears profusely, and sends the most unfriendly sign language your way as he speeds up alongside you to see the whites of your eyes as he continues to heap epithets upon you. What we're suggesting is that one possibility is that people who respond reactively in this way may have underdeveloped prefrontal lobes. Cut a more developed person off on the highway and he may honk at you and be angry briefly, but his impulse control kicks in and he remains in control.

PUBERTY

By the age of 16, in most cases, the hormonal changes and their emotional and physical impacts on the young bodies of our early adolescents are complete. This chemical "settling down" of sorts paves the way for the late adolescent to turn his attentions to his social development, and most importantly to his future as he anticipates college or whatever he's going to pursue beyond high school. Effectively relating to others, and the ability to create and sustain more mature relationships, romantic or otherwise, also emerge in the wake of puberty.

SOCIAL MOBILITY

A certain transformation occurs the moment a teenager or his friends are handed the keys to the family car. The teen is no longer restricted to his home and neighborhood. He now can essentially pick up and go where he wants to when he wants to; this provides substantially more independence. He may also hold down a part-time job during this period, adding to his ability to assume increased responsibilities and "try on" roles in the workplace as he anticipates career choices in his future.

CHILDHOOD'S END

The late adolescent period marks the end of childhood. During the first stage of adolescence, young people are moving away from childhood things, but have not left them entirely behind. For example, many 13-through-15-year-olds may still dress up at Halloween and go door to door, whereas most teens just a year or so older wouldn't be caught dead doing such a thing. Also, more 13-through-15-year-olds are involved with team sports and clubs than their older counterparts. Television cartoon viewing drops off to a degree at age 16 as tastes mature and with the late-teen's increased ability to get out of the house.

The implications of these shifts away from the trappings and activities of childhood are significant. For most product and program categories, kid-targeting developers and marketers cannot assume the 16-through-19-year-old as a target. He is essentially an adult in most respects when it comes to the types of programs he now prefers and the types of products he chooses to buy and use. Should a company wish to target the 16-through-19-year-old directly, another segmentation discussion needs to be had outside the parameters of a book on kid marketing such as this one—a discussion regarding what approach to take to getting at the lifestyles, the perceptions, the preferences of the late-adolescent "almost adult."

Some products and programs do hold older teens' interests and remain viable. Electronic games, for example, remain popular, especially with males, because of their high level of complexity and competitive challenge. As has been stated earlier, older teens tend to prefer sophisticated role-playing games such as *Myst* and realistic sports games. TV shows such as sitcoms and soap-opera-like dramas that star teens and young adults also maintain their popularity throughout the teen years, as do movies featuring slapstick and teenage humor and action-adventure films.

This older teen has, from a kid-marketing perspective, "outgrown" almost all the other categories of kid-targeted products and programs. He is essentially beyond childhood and now enjoys the tastes and preferences of young adulthood. Let's look at some of the 16-through-19-year-old's changing preferences.

TOYS AND GAMES: The "toys" that remain of interest to older teens are sports "toys" such as Frisbees, Nerf Balls to be played with in the park or at the beach, rollerblades, and sports equipment. "Electronic toys" such as calculators, electronic address books, portable radios, and CD players remain popular as well. Electronic games remain popular, as has been noted. Board and card games that are sufficiently "adult" in their themes, such as chess, Scrabble, and Trivial Pursuit, and card games such as poker remain somewhat popular, but the 16-through-19-year-old is typically so involved with her school and social interests that many of these activities diminish their draw during this period.

MOVIES: Humorous and action-oriented films remain popular throughout the teen years. In fact movie makers recognize the huge importance of the teen and young-adult markets for their films. Demographic data points to the fact that the 13-through-19-year-old is the most frequent moviegoer. The essential difference in taste between the 13-through-15-year-old and older teens is that the late adolescent is more likely to be drawn toward more such adult themes as romantic comedies and serious dramas that emphasize human and romantic relationships—as well as to maintain an ongoing interest in comedies and action-adventure themes.

TELEVISION: The television viewing preferences of the late-adolescent are essentially the same as for the early-adolescent—an interest in sitcoms such as *Home Improvement, Friends,* and *Seinfeld* and in dramas such as *ER.* Maturing teens are, however, increasingly interested in social and political issues. They also regularly view cable educational shows, network news shows, sensationalized realistic TV shows such as *COPS* and *Emergency 911,* talk shows, and even such in-depth news shows as *20/20* and *60 Minutes.*

PUBLICATIONS: In the arena of magazines and other printed texts, we see pronounced changes that reflect the shift from the early-adolescent, leaving-childhood-behind stage to the "almost adult" late adolescent stage. *Sports Illustrated for Kids,* for example, and other kid-targeted magazines such as *Disney Adventures* and *Boys' Life* will be supplanted by regular adult fare such as *People* and the adult *Sports Illustrated.* Specialty publications, however, such as *Nintendo Power* and its Sega equivalent will sustain their draw. The increase of reading on-line materials also cannot be ignored in today's electronic era. The reading of fiction or nonfiction books, newspaper reading, and reading serious newsmagazines such as *Time* and *Newsweek* will also be on the rise for the 16+ year-old, although levels of readership will still remain low until more maturation sets in.

MUSIC: Musical tastes will shift also during this late-adolescent period away from teeny-bopper and simple rap music and toward mainstream adult performers. By this time, individual tastes and preferences are well established, and musical subgenres that exist (such as Heavy Metal, Rap, Country, Hard Rock, Soft Rock, and Pop) each have their magnetism for segments of the 16+ target cohort.

FOOD AND BEVERAGES: Most grocery-store- or convenience-store-bought items are of the adult variety by the time our youth reaches this late-adolescent period. In the safety of her own home, our 16-through-19-year-old will still consume a goodly amount of cartoon-character-populated kid or all-family-targeted cereals, snacks, and beverages, but overall she has migrated to purely adult tastes. Importantly, this late adolescent has both more money to spend and increased opportunities for independent purchasing. What she purchases with that money, moreover, is more likely to be adult-targeted in nature, and much less likely to be child-targeted, than ever before.

FAST FOOD: While most fast-food establishments remain quite popular with this age group, the late adolescent will tend to have a slight preference for the more adult-appearing fast-food establishments over those such as McDonald's that might be perceived as young-kid targeted, with their kiddish characters and play areas. Quality of food is also a big issue with this older, more discriminating "almost adult."

OTHER CATEGORIES: For other categories, such as software, apparel, and personal hygiene, her/his tastes, preferences, and buying patterns are almost completely young adult or adult.

WINNERS

In previous chapters we have isolated one or two "megahits" for each of the age segments. Given that the 16-through-19-year-old is really beyond kid-targeting for the most part, it's difficult to isolate a kid-targeted product or program and label it a megahit for this age segment. Indeed, this chapter is abbreviated because of this fact, although it is important to briefly explore how the 16-through-19-year-old's needs, neurology, cognition, perceptions, moral sense, and humor styles have progressed and changed: Compare the list below to similar lists in preceding chapters.

Common Denominators (16 Through 19)

Needs	Love, peer involvement and approval, success, increased independence, and autonomy
Neurology	R System—Brain stem (ages 0–7) M System—Limbic (ages 1–11) C System—Cortex—Right hemisphere (ages 4–15) Structuring and "entrainment" of the brain is essentially completed during this late teen period.
Cognition	Logical operations, increasingly able to perform complex and abstract tasks
Perceptual	Reality and detail, higher ability to discriminate
Moral Sense	Postconventional; increased ability to decide for oneself between good and bad, right and wrong, aesthetics
Self/Social	Increased independence from parents and peers, increased mobility
Humor	Slapstick, action, dark side; increased ability to understand subtleties, e.g., innuendo, puns, sarcasm, irony

NEEDS

The late adolescent is developing a more intense need to *succeed* in that he is anticipating being "on his own" in short order. At the same time, although his need for parental and peer *acceptance* is still in place, he has matured (if all has gone well) to a point of more independent thought and is needing this outside acceptance less.

NEUROLOGY AND COGNITION

Given a healthy and continuous brain development up to this point, the 16-to-19-year-old's brain is almost completely developed by late adolescence. His cognitive functions are ideally fully in place at this point, allowing him to deal with complex problems at a high level of abstraction. (It's important to again note that this is the *ideal* scenario. Indications are that a percentage of our young people—due to trauma or drugs, or to lack of early parental love and bonding—have not developed full brain/cognitive capacity. A study of incoming freshmen at Brandeis University,[4] for example, showed that an alarming number—as many as 50 percent—of these freshmen were not able to demonstrate mastery of what Piaget[5] refers to as "formal operations," i.e., advanced abstract reasoning—the kind of reasoning ability, for example, needed to solve algebraic word problems.)

PERCEPTION

As can be seen from Figure 8.1 below, the perceptual filter or window that the 16-to-19-year-old is looking through is focused to a great degree on his future, i.e., his relationships and his career.

FIGURE 8.1 A MODEL OF THE PERCEPTUAL FILTER OF THE 16-THROUGH-19-YEAR-OLD

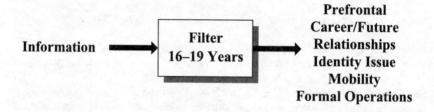

Because his cognitive abilities are now advanced, he is also better equipped to think things through and examine the different sides of the issues that confront him.

THE MORAL SENSE

More effectively than ever before, the 16+ year-old—because of his developing prefrontal lobe—can utilize his cognitive skills to make choices between right and wrong and good and bad. This does not mean, of course, that his choices will all be the right ones, but his ability to discriminate between options, think logically, problem-solve, self-reflect, and "put himself in the shoes of others" greatly enhances his ability to effectively exercise his morality.

SELF/SOCIAL DEVELOPMENT

Most importantly, the late adolescent is (ideally) functioning as a more autonomous human being at this point. He does not need the acceptance of others to the same degree that he did during the previous two stages of development, and this allows for a significantly greater degree of self-determination. Ideally he has transitioned from an *external locus of con-*

trol to an *internal locus of control.* This term refers to where a person looks in order to determine choices. Does he look outside himself to his family and peers and society at large to tell him what he should feel, think, do? Or does he look inward, to himself? Ideally, the 16-through-19-year-old is healthily turning toward internality.

HUMOR

The 16-through-19-year-old's increased social maturation and cognitive development results in a more sophisticated sense of humor. This age youth will tend to move away from simple slapstick and other childish forms of humor and toward more sophisticated humor such as that found in more adult comedy TV shows and movies. With his increased cognitive abilities he can understand and appreciate all forms of advanced humor including puns, innuendo, irony, and sarcasm and will prefer these to simpler comedic fare.

SUMMARY

The 16-through-19-year-old is essentially completing his transition away from childhood and is a "young adult" in terms of his tastes, preferences, and purchasing patterns. Let's return once again to the elements present in the YMS Product Leverage Matrix—Figure 8.2—to confirm this young-adult status.

MEDIUM/PRODUCTS: Many product categories that appeal to the late adolescent are mainstream adult products. By now, the 16+ year-old is reading adult magazines for the most part, watching adult TV shows, and buying adult-targeted foods and beverages. There are certain young-adult–targeted entertainment products and programs that will catch his eye—for example, TV programming such as MTV, complete with its array of sexy music videos and dark-side humor like that of *Beavis and Butt-Head,* young-adult–targeted music, and certain music-related publications such as *Rolling Stone* and other youth-targeted publications such as *Mad* magazine, *Seventeen,* and *YM* [*Young and Modern*]. By the time these young adults move through their twenties they will be leaving many of these young-adult preferences behind as well.

CONCEPT AND CONTENT: Compared to what will be their more conservative tastes in Concept and Content in later years, these 16+ year-olds are marked by their preference for innovative and sometimes

FIGURE 8.2: THE PRODUCT LEVERAGE MATRIX

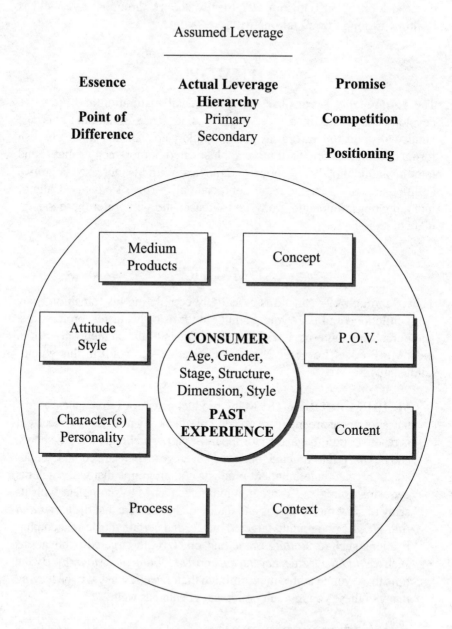

controversial concepts and content. It is this "taste" that keeps shows like *Married with Children*, MTV *Music Videos, Duckman,* and *Beavis and Butt-Head* on the air. Many older teens, in their quest for independence of thought, are attracted to these irreverent and sometimes "taboo" concepts because of their raw and iconoclastic content.

However, it's important to keep in mind that the above allusion to preferences for edgy and controversial content does not apply to every single older teen. As in any segment of society, there are some youths who for religious or other reasons are extremely conservative in their tastes and preferences—and many more who are in-between.

POINT OF VIEW AND ATTITUDE/STYLE: For most older teens, their "P.O.V." or point of view is less conservative and tends more toward the experimental, innovative, and sometimes controversial. They are attracted to variety and experimentation in Attitude/Style— in apparel, in the graphic presentation of product packaging, and in the execution of TV programming and films. The so-called "generation gap" is quite evident here, as many late adolescents push away from the conservative and the traditional and move toward innovative and iconoclastic elements that offer them a chance to create their own unique identity.

CHARACTERS/PERSONALITIES: While still being entertained by the sophomoric humor of personalities such as Jim Carrey or by the slapstick antics of the Road Runner and Wile E. Coyote, Garfield, and Bugs Bunny, the characters and personalities that primarily attract the 16-through-19-year-old are more adult—the Sly Stallones, the Michael Jordans, the Mariah Careys, the Sharon Stones, the Dennis Rodmans, the Madonnas, and yes, even the Bill Clintons.

CONTEXT: *Context* essentially refers to time and place. With full cognitive function in place, any combinations of time contexts can be appreciated: past-based shows, future-based shows or films, flashbacks, etc. In the same vein, any and all geographical contexts can be utilized, from foreign locales to past or futuristic and sci-fi fantasy locales.

PROCESS: *Process* refers to such elements as pacing, special musical, sound, and visual effects, the utilization of novel approaches to timing, and innovative formats. In terms of process preferences, the 16-through-19-year-old has been conditioned, just as his younger counterparts have been, to appreciate and prefer faster-paced programming and advertising, lots of special effects, multiple visual images, and more complex combinations of elements.

ON TO THE BATTLE OF THE SEXES

With this chapter we conclude our in-depth and specific look at the different age segments that a kid-targeting product or program developer or marketer needs to understand. In the next chapter we turn our attention toward gender. Just what are the differences between the sexes as children mature through these different stages of development? How should these differences be taken into account? Let's see.

CHAPTER 9

GENDER DIFFERENCES
Barbie® Meets Godzilla®

> Men and women are not only biologically and anatomi-
> cally different, they are psychologically different as well.
> For example, it is universally observed that, compared to
> men, women are more intuitive . . . and are more inter-
> ested in love and relationships. . . .
>
> —John Gray, Ph.D.,
> *Men, Women and Relationships*[1]

As we approach the millennium, the controversy over the similarities and differences between males and females rages on. Are girls predetermined by genetics and biology to prefer Barbie® dolls over Godzilla® monster action figures? Are boys predetermined by their physiology to prefer to play with GIJoe stuff rather than play tea party? While no one would dare argue that there are no differences between boys and girls—given the obvious differences in their physical makeups—the battle still is being fought over nature versus nurture. To what degree are gender differences a product of heredity and to what degree are they a product of learning that takes place in the child's environment?

The discussion is an important one, given that each year hundreds of thousands if not millions of dollars are invested in trying to develop female interest in traditionally male toys and games and—to a much lesser extent—to develop male interest in traditionally female products and programs. For example, when Mattel's action-figure-line phenomenon, *Masters of the Universe,* starring He-Man, rose to stardom in the 1980s among boys, Mattel with its She-Ra and other companies such as Galoob with its Golden Girls action figures attempted for the most part unsuccessfully to lure girls into action-figure play. Currently we find toy companies and game companies alike researching ways to bring more girls into the electronic-game-player fold. Currently girls make up approximately 20 percent of the electronic-game-*playing* audience; often they are playing games purchased by siblings or friends, or to a much lesser degree games that they have *purchased themselves* or asked parents for.

The financial reasons for these efforts are obvious. Given that there are as many girls out there in the marketplace as boys, manufacturers' profits would increase substantially if they could penetrate both boy and girl markets.

THE RESEARCH ON GENDER DIFFERENCES

Thousands of research studies have been conducted on sex and gender and their influences on human behavior. Most of these studies point to nature or genetics as the primary factor influencing behavior, with the researchers (mostly men) citing hormonal differences, such as differences in testosterone levels between males and females, as a reality that leads to behavioral differences and preferences. For example, given that the higher presence of testosterone in males has been shown to lead to their increased aggressive tendencies, it would only be natural that boys would prefer aggressive toys such as action figures over dolls.

And there's more. Much more. A great many studies point to specific physiological and behavioral differences between the sexes. Some of the findings are listed below.

MALES

By age 3 or 4, males are more intrepid explorers: males tend to be more original and inventive in toy-play patterns. Given ordinary wooden alphabet blocks, for example, boys will explore and invent more possibilities of how to play with them than will girls.

More creative males have been reported by teachers as more disruptive.

Creativity scores for young males are higher than for females the same age.

Assertiveness is higher in young males.

Physical differences between males and females in height, weight, fat and hair distribution, body contour, bone structure, and muscular development are easily observable.

Growth and development are programmed differently in males and females. Male fetuses grow faster and male infants are both heavier and "taller."

Male muscular structure is larger and more powerful.

Male hearts are larger and lungs have greater vital capacity.

Males' basal metabolic rate is higher.

Male physical strength is greater, and their handgrip is twice as strong as that of females.

Systolic blood pressure is higher in males, which allows the cardiovascular system to better adapt to stress and physical exertion.

Male blood has a greater amount of hemoglobin, and as a result can carry more oxygen.

Males are more efficient at eliminating metabolites such as lactic acid, which is a by-product of muscular activity.

Males possess superior visuospatial abilities. After a few weeks of age, boys will attend more readily to visual patterns than girls.

From birth on, the body movements of males are more vigorous, gross, and global than those of females.

Males are more proficient in mathematical, mechanical, and visuospatial skills.

Regarding the behavior of adult males toward boy and girl babies, male adults interact differently with male babies than with female babies, being more physical and aggressive with boy babies and more cautious and gentle with girls.

FEMALES

Female sensorimotor skills are quite different from those of males. Females are more sensitive to touch, pain, and sound, and throughout life they are better able to localize sounds and differentiate between their intensities.

After a few weeks of age, females will attend more to sound and tonal patterns than to visual patterns.

Females are more responsive from birth on to the sound of other babies crying.

From birth on, females' body movements are finer and more confined to small muscle groups than are males'.

On the whole, female babies are quieter and more placid, while male babies are more fretful and irritable.

Females' perceptual abilities are less efficient than males' in mechanical relationships and visuospatial skills.

Females score higher on areas of intelligence tests that demand verbal fluency and short-term memory.

Females exhibit more finger speed and dexterity.

Females demonstrate fewer extremes in almost all phases of testing: intelligence; physical, biological, and academic categories; deviancy; and personality.

Females exhibit more empathic behaviors.

By age 3, females are more responsive to new playmates.

Females have better clarity and quality of speech throughout childhood than males.

Females show greater childhood interest in playmates than in objects.

Females demonstrate more accurate understanding of social cues.

Females are faster in their processing of verbal information.

Adult females—mothers—behave differently toward their male babies than toward their female babies. They are more likely to look at their sons and physically pacify them, whereas they spend more time talking to their daughters.

ANOTHER POINT OF VIEW

Possibly the most comprehensive work ever completed on the subject of gender takes a different view. Linda Brannon, in her 1996 book, *Gender: Psychological Perspectives,* relying on almost 1,000 referenced sources, suggests that there are "maximalist" views and "minimalist" views on the subject.[2] The maximalist view is that there are many inherent differences between men and women and these many differences lead to major differences in preferences, behavior, and choices in life. The minimalist view is that there are minor substantive differences between males and females—but most preferences, behaviors, and life choices are far more a question of nurture—that is, they are formed by environmental and learning influences. After her own thorough and comprehensive research, Brannon clearly comes out on the side of the minimalists, claiming that many of the studies to date are male-biased and based on ex post facto reasoning.

The controversy, however, is far from resolved. Studies and articles attending to this controversy abound. A few of these are cited below.

USE OF BRAIN SPACE: A March 27, 1995 *Newsweek* article entitled "Gray Matters" explains how men and women use their brains differently. For example, when asked to "think of nothing," men had more activity in their temporal limbic system, an evolutionarily ancient brain region that controls emotions linked to action, especially aggression. On the other side of the gender fence, when women were asked to think of nothing they had more activity in the cingulate gyrus, an evolutionarily recent region that controls complex expressions of emotions, such as showing anger by looks, not punches. These studies also revealed that when women feel sad, they use as much as eight times more gray matter in the feeling process than men do. This does not suggest that women have the capacity to feel sadder than men, just that they use more of their brains in the feeling process. The implication for female children is that more of their actual physiology, specifically brain space, may be dedicated to and involved in emotional processing.

THE CORPUS CALLOSUM: A March 14, 1995, *USA Today* article entitled "Battle of Sexes Starts in the Brain" details findings based on MRI brain scans, which can actually watch the brain functioning. Some of those findings, along with autopsy studies, indicate that the corpus callosum—the mass of fibers connecting the brain's right and left hemispheres—is larger in proportion to brain weight in women than in men. More information is apparently being exchanged between the two hemispheres in women: this *could* account for women's greater verbal skills and possibly even explain "women's intuition." Another difference noted in this article: a woman's brain has emotional capacities on both sides or hemispheres of the brain, whereas a man's emotional capacities are centered in the right hemisphere.

TOYS ARE WHO? In a January 4, 1996 *Los Angeles Times* article headed "The Story on Toys for Girls—They're Mostly About Boys," journalist Megan Rosenfeld cites a 1993 study which found that eleven of the fifteen most advertised toys were intended for boys. And another study showed that seven toy aisles at Toys 'R' Us were ". . . crammed with things for boys while five aisles of mostly dolls were for girls." Feminists will certainly bridle at what else Ms. Rosenfeld discovered. She suggests that in their attempts to create more toys and games targeted to girls, toy and game companies concluded after talking with lots of girls that in order to appeal to girls they had to focus their toys and games around—guess who?—boys! Rosenfeld writes: "There is occasional reference to a career, or being smart, but the overriding theme of "games such as *Sealed With A Kiss* . . . is that a girl should be pretty, plot how to get, keep or trade a boyfriend, go shopping, gossip, paint her toenails and her face, and kiss, kiss, kiss. And her primary colors are pink and purple."

Sexual and gender stereotypes abound. Rosenfeld offers a case in point: Disney's feature film *Toy Story,* in which girls are given ". . . very short shrift. Bo Peep is the female toy that comes to life, all batting eyelashes and sexy voice, and her only action is to smother the cowboy with kisses. The little girl in the film has a tea party with her dolls."

So the controversy continues. After all the research is reviewed and all is said and done to attempt to establish a clear winner in the "battle of the sexes," it can only safely be assumed that there are:

a. genetic and biological differences,
    and also
b. cultural, environmental, and learning differences.

No doubt, the relationship between the two is symbiotic. That is, nature influences and has an impact on nurture, *and* nurture influences and has an impact on nature, over time.

NOW WHAT?

One would have to turn one's back on reality to deny, whether it can be laid at the doorstep of nature or nurture, that there *are* significant differences in preferences, in attitudes, in play patterns, and in behavior patterns between boys and girls. In a recent ABC special entitled *Boys and Girls ARE Different,* many of these differences were enumerated. For example, give little boys and little girls Barbie® dolls and boys will find a way to play sword-fight with them, whereas girls will change their clothes and apply makeup to them.

At YMS Consulting we have studied the many differences between boys and girls as they relate to specific play activities or Play Patterns, Character Identification, and even Contexts or favorite settings—Contexts that girls prefer as distinct from Contexts that boys prefer. Differences also evolve as children mature and grow through the different stages of development that we have been outlining in this book. In the following, therefore, we approach each of the age segments separately and list in detail the differences that we have discovered.

AGES BIRTH THROUGH 2

One might think that before the age of 3 children are relatively asexual in their behaviors. Not so, according to many studies. There are some telling and quite observable differences even at this early stage. Girls, for example, tend to maintain eye contact with Mom and Dad longer than boys, who tend to look off into space more. When building with blocks, most boys build upward, creating tower-like structures (which they then knock down), whereas girls tend to build outward, suggesting protective structures such as fences, houses, and walls.

FAVORITE PLAY ACTIVITIES

Given the sensorimotor stage of development of the birth-through-2-year-old, he/she is intensely involved in the exploration of and learning about his/her environment and in gaining an emotionally secure base. Play activities for both boys and girls, therefore, center around the next two areas.

MANIPULATION AND EXPERIENCING: Playing—tactilely, orally, visually—with objects of all kinds, including his own and others' fingers, toes, hair, eyes, and other body parts; toys; mobiles; things in nature—in short everything and anything he can get his senses on.

BONDING, LOVE, AND SAFETY: The act of "play" with Mom and other nurturing adults and caretakers.

CHARACTER IDENTIFICATION

The birth-through-2-year-old is not yet ready cognitively to relate meaningfully or "identify" with most of the characters in his home or school or in the media. Most "characters" or role models, such as firemen or sports stars, are quite abstract and future-oriented for the birth-through-2-year-old. There are a few exceptions toward the older end of this age range: characters in the child's immediate environment, such as stuffed animals and TV characters like Barney and Big Bird—big and loving animals that provide fun, stimulation, and love. Importantly, there does not appear to be any *significant* gender difference in how little girls or little boys relate to these loving characters.

FAVORITE SETTINGS OR CONTEXTS

One could hypothesize that birth-through-2-year-old males might prefer more object-filled and action-oriented play spaces whereas girls might prefer calmer, more people-oriented spaces, but there is no known evidence to indicate any significant difference in settings or locales preferred by boys or by girls. We know of no studies that have looked at, for example, the possibility that little boys prefer settings such as the outdoors (where they can be more aggressive) over safer indoor settings preferred by little girls. Given their limited mobility, both girls and boys in this age range will likely "prefer" the safety of home.

"Contexts," as it is used here, also refers to favorite themes that children relate to. In storybooks, for example, 2-year-old females may differ from their little male contemporaries in their preferences for softer, less aggressive themes.

AGES 3 THROUGH 7

By the time our boys and girls have reached the age of 3, a great many sexual/gender differences are starting to appear. In a related matter, research shows, for example, that one's own gender identity, that is, the realization that one is a boy or a girl, occurs at approximately 3 years of age. In the listings below we see a great many differences in play activities, character identification, and context preferences emerging. As you examine each set of differences between the preferred play activities, characters, and contexts of males and females, look for the patterns or tendencies listed below.

1. Male play is more aggressive; female play is less aggressive and gentler.
2. Female play is more relationship-centered and more nurturing; male play is more object-centered.
3. Male play is more gross motor involved; female play often involves more fine motor skills, e.g., dressing dolls, making jewelry, and other crafts.
4. Male play often revolves around building—digging, constructing; female play involves arranging and organizing.
5. Males identify with heroic male characters; females tend to identify with both male and female role models and heroes.
6. Males tend to prefer themes and contexts directly associated with their more aggressive forms of play such as sports, action-figure play scenarios, and more "dangerous" themes such as dinosaurs and monsters. Females tend to prefer less aggressive, safer scenarios.

Favorite Play Activities, Ages 3 Through 7: Males

Dramatic play of store, train, hospital	Play with pets
Rides tricycle, climbs, does "tricks"	Block play, attempting detailed construc-
Draws, paints, colors	tions, Legos
Plays fort and house	Potato head play
Beginning roller skating	Running, skipping, swinging, jumping
Play with tools	Games matching pictures and forms
Simple carpentry, hammering	Mechanical and simple electronic toys
Male action figures	Ball play: tossing, bouncing, throwing,
Games of pretend	batting, fielding, kicking
Magnetic drawing boards	Accumulating (collecting) lots of stuff
Simple magic, tricks, jigsaw puzzles	Digging holes and tunnels
Simple game play	Play with wagons, trains, trucks, airplanes,
Bicycles	boats
Swimming	Trading cards
Simple model airplanes, other vehicles	Rigging items
Building tree houses, tent play	Pretend gun play, fighting games, war play
Plush animals (up to age 5)	Beginning interest in "adult" ideas toward
Colorforms, color books	top of this age range, e.g., chemistry,
Ride-On vehicles	navigation
Hand puppets, other puppets (up to 5)	Paint sets

Favorite Play Activities, Ages 3 Through 7: Females

Dramatic play with other children
Imaginary companion play
Nurturing doll play, doll houses
Jump rope
Beginning roller skating
Play with Kittens, Puppies
Copying letters and numbers
Simple table games
Printing letters to spell "real" words
Play school, library
Jewelry play
"Like Me" doll play
Transitional object play: plush, blankies, etc.
Stuffed animals
Paint sets
Cooking sets
Cooking/kitchen play
"Secret" activities (Sweet Secrets)

Play house, store, hospital, costume, props
Drawing, painting, coloring
Draping of furniture for house play
Sewing
Painting, drawing, coloring, cutting, pasting
Dress-up: adult clothes
Clay play
Imaginative play: Playing horse
Fancy goods, i.e., Hello Kitty
Hopscotch, ball play
Fashion doll play
Lite Brite concepts
Ponies, horses
Colorforms, stickers
Ride-On toys
Hand puppets (ages 3–5)
Elaboration of doll play, e.g., with accessories: clothes, suitcases

Character Identification, Ages 3 Through 7: Males

Firemen
Teachers
Train engineers
Princes
Kings
Martial arts
Good father
Sports stars
Wacky scientists
Adventurers
Magicians

Knights
Soldiers
Policemen
Superhuman (He-Man, wrestlers, Incredible Hulk, Mighty Morphin Power Rangers, Hercules)
Uncle and Gramps
Doctors
Humorous animal characters: Bugs Bunny, Garfield, etc.
Disidentification with villains

Character Identification, Ages 3 Through 7: Females

Fashion doll archetypes: Barbie®
Ballerinas
Dancers
Mother
Teachers
Magic/Magician
Fashion models
Horse trainer/keeper
Brides
Aerobic teacher

Babies: (Muppet Babies)
Good Fairies
Queens, Princesses
Big sisters
Nurses
Entertainment icon/Celebrity: Actress/Singer
Ice skaters
Elegant debutantes
Cooks/chefs
Disidentification with villains

Favorite Settings or Contexts, Ages 3 Through 7: Males

Zoo	Other planets
Jungle	School
Hospital	Fire station
Police station	Store
Carnival	Circus
Post office	Neighborhood
Outer space	Playground
Prehistoric	Railroad station
Beach	Construction site
Auto raceway	Auto racetrack
Farm	Car, Garage, Gas station
Toy stores	Martial arts studio
Amusement Parks: Disneyland, Magic Mountain, Knott's Berry Farm	

Favorite Settings or Contexts, Ages 3 Through 7: Females

Home	School
Friend's house	The stage
Castles	Fashion shows
Dance studios	Circus
Ranches	Farmyard
Dollhouses	Elegant balls
Fantasy Island	Neighborhood
Animalland	Beaches
Toy stores	Parks, nature preserves
Amusement parks with children's themes	

AGES 8 THROUGH 12

As can easily be concluded from a close look at the play preferences, favorite characters, and favorite settings of males aged 3 through 7 as compared with females, the 3-through-7-year-old boy lives and traffics in a somewhat different "world" than the 3-through-7-year-old girl. This trend continues throughout the 8-through-12 developmental stage, as illustrated in the following list.

Favorite Play Activities, Ages 8 Through 12: Males

Video games	Collecting and arranging collections
TV viewing	"Hanging out"
Cartoons/animation	Model making
Comic books (i.e., X-men)	Group sports: baseball, football, soccer
Jigsaw puzzles, map puzzles	Organized clubs
Challenge games (scorn simplicity)	Bike riding
Gadget age, fine motor complexity	Electric trains

Hiking
Responding to ads
Personalized mail and communications
Numbering, classifying, counting money
Drawing, designing, creating
Pets
Reading
Photography
Nature interest/Ecology
Collecting, e.g., stamps, bottle caps, coins, post cards, trading cards
Seasonal interest, e.g., Flying kites
Concerts, music events
Board and card games
Inventing
Tools for repairs (bike, athletic equipment)

Skateboarding
Rollerblades
Chemistry sets, more complex formulas
Use of telegraph, walkie-talkie
Computer games
Computer graphics
Complex challenge games (e.g., Dungeons and Dragons)
Video rentals
Drawing maps
Collecting catalogs
Internet/e-mail
Advanced construction (Erector Sets, Legos)
Jet rockets, aircraft, boats, cars
Companionship play

Play Activities, Ages 8 Through 12: Females

Group and companionship play
Going to the movies
Jigsaws, maps, puzzles
Video games
Dramatic play: producing shows
Collecting and arranging collections
Secret and organized clubs
Advanced doll play (relationships)
Adult relationships
Cooking, baking
Mall browsing
Sewing
Making lists of collections, Christmas lists, etc.
Numbering, classifying, counting money
Nature interests
Communication (Internet, e-mail, telephone)
"Girl talk"

Music events, concerts
Video rentals
Swimming, track and field
Horses and horseback riding
Pets
Dressing and clothes
Painting
Ceramics
Fashion design (computer designing)
Writing stories, plays
Drawing
Photography
Bike riding
Roller skates
Jump rope
Shopping
Ecology concerns/nature study
Spectator sports
TV viewing

Character Identification, Ages 8 Through 12: Males

Action heroes (e.g., Arnold Schwarzenegger, Bruce Willis, Sylvester Stallone, Bruce Lee, Batman, Superman)
Power figures (e.g., X-Men)
Martial arts experts
Pro sports stars (e.g., Michael Jordan, John Elway, Wayne Gretzky)
Medieval characters (knights, etc.)
Political figures

Soldiers
Underwater, deep-sea heroes (Seals, etc.)
Adolescents
Old West figures (Wyatt Earp, Doc Holliday)
Rugged individualists (Tom Sawyer, Huck Finn)
Cartoon characters
TV and film stars

Music stars
Teachers
Parents
Coaches
Race-car drivers

Game hunters, explorers
Famous historical figures
Older brothers and older brothers' friends
Astronauts

Character Identification, Ages 8 Through 12: Females

Actresses/movie stars
Male and female sports celebrities
Male and female political figures
Music celebrities
Figure-skating stars (Nancy Kerrigan)
"Knights in shining armor," rescuers, e.g.,
    Baywatch lifeguards
Models
"Hunks"
Dancers
Talented and strong girls of own age

Cartoon characters
Teachers
Parents
TV prime-time and soap-opera stars
Adolescents
"Successful" women
Older sisters and friends
Track-and-field stars
Gymnasts
Cartoon characters

Favorite Settings and Contexts, Ages 8 Through 12: Males

Rollerblading locales
Surfing beaches
Skate-boarding areas
BMX racing
Karate/martial arts
Ranch/Old West
Olympic events
Outer space
School/home
Urban locales, i.e., "the street"
Caves
Hiking/mountains
Secret rooms, space, e.g., attics
Ocean/underwater
Amusement parks
Police/Crime settings
The desert
Adventure in foreign lands—Jungle
Laboratories
Army, Navy, Marines, Air Force
Deserted islands
Prehistoric (dinosaurs)
Beach

Auto racetracks
Monster cars/trucks/stunt cars
Seaworld, water parks
The zoo
School club
Concerts/Amphitheaters
Malls
Movie theaters
Convenience stores
Parties
Street carnivals
Urban park
Basketball courts
Dining-out locations
Caves
Music or video stores
War settings
Castles
Circus
Pirate ships
Submarines
Boxing/Wrestling ring

Favorite Settings and Contexts, Ages 8 Through 12: Females

School	Historical settings: Old South, Old West,
Friend's house	etc.
The stage	School club
Club, clubhouse	Malls
Mountains	Movie theaters
Ranches	Convenience stores
Fashion shows	Elegant events/balls
Horse-related settings	Yachts
Skating rinks	Parties
Dance studios	Street carnivals
Aerobics studios	Athletic events
Weddings	Urban scenes (parks, street)
Circuses	Music/video stores
Castles	Dining-out locations
Beaches	Bodies of water, e.g., an ocean, a lake
Haunted houses	Olympics
Laboratories	Deserts
Islands	The ballet
Foreign lands	Concerts/Amphitheaters
Jungles	Under water
Zoos	Sea World, water parks
Amusement parks	Slumber parties

AGES 13 THROUGH 15

As male and female children enter into their teen years there are dramatic changes in the types of play activities they engage in, the types of characters that they model themselves after, and the kinds of settings and themes they prefer. A common thread throughout these changes is a shift away from fantasy-related play, characters and settings and toward reality-based activities, characters, and contexts. "Play" is rapidly being replaced by goal-oriented activities such as organized sports, religious and school club activities, and just hanging out with and communicating with friends. The types of personalities and characters that the 13-through-15-year-old relates most strongly to are more realistic (e.g., a Michael Jordan rather than a Batman), and favorite settings and themes are now in the real world more than in the fantasy world.

Another important conclusion that can be arrived at by an analysis of the favorite play activities, characters, and settings/themes listed below for the 13-through-15-year-old male and female is that in many cases they are converging back, showing more similarities between the sexes than differences. While there remain substantial differences, these differences are not so pronounced as they were for the 8-through-12 year old. This is particularly striking when we look at favorite settings/themes for 13-through-15-year-old males and females.

Favorite Play Activities, Ages 13 Through 15: Males

Video games	Sci-Fi
Martial arts	Playing cards
Dining out	Electronic games
Entertaining at home	Listening to music
Watching TV/Videos	Going shopping
Going to movies	Team sports: football, basketball, baseball,
"Hanging Out"	track, soccer
Surfing	Skateboarding
Collections (baseball cards, etc.)	Rollerblading
"Street"/playground sports	Camping/Hiking
Bike riding	Advanced model-building
Ecology/nature study	Graphics, design, drawing, painting, sculp-
Reading books	ture
Auto mechanics	Table games, cards, scrapbooks
Social clubs	Puzzles/maps
Concerts	Seasonal sports: skiing, swimming
Tools, woodworking	Boys' clubs: Scouts, religion, sports
Music lessons/playing	Amusement parks
Listening to radio	Reading magazines
Getting/sending direct mail	Using computers
Photography/video recording	Dance/go dancing
Board games	Internet/e-mail (computer communication)
Baseball cards	Comic books (*The X-Men*)
Sports in general	

Favorite Play Activities, Ages 13 Through 15: Females

Going to movies	Watching TV
Dining out	Playing cards
Dancing/going out dancing	Billiards/pool
Shopping	Team sports: basketball, volleyball,
Ceramics, sculpture, painting	softball, soccer
Bike riding	Hanging out
Tennis	Swimming
Roller skating, rollerblading	Gymnastics
Pets	Surfing
The mall	Horseback riding
Social clubs	Nature/ecology
Video games	Design, drawing, graphics
Concerts	Listening to radio
Beach	Amusement parks
Getting/sending direct mail	Mountains
Board games	Internet/e-mail (computer communication)

Character Identification, Ages 13 Through 15: Males

Sports celebrities	TV stars
Movie stars	Political figures
News commentators	Race-car drivers
Religious/spiritual teachers	Producers/directors
Action heroes	Talk-show hosts
Cartoon characters	Parents
Comedians	Coaches
Teachers	Music celebrities
Female "bombshells"	

Character Identification, Ages 13 Through 15: Females

Sports celebrities (male and female)	Comedians
Movie stars	"Hunks" (attractive males)
Soap stars	TV celebrities
Cartoon characters	Talk-show hosts
Strong females in leadership positions	News commentators
Teachers	Religious/spiritual teachers
Parents	Political figures
Music celebrities	Models

Favorite Settings and Contexts, Ages 13 Through 15: Males

Sporting events	Pool/Billiard locations
Video arcades	Concerts/Amphitheaters
School	Malls
Raves/Party scenes	Dining-out locations
Urban parks, basketball courts	Movie theaters
Beaches	Convenience stores
Mountains	Street carnivals
Auto racetracks	Music/video stores
Ocean/underwater	School events
Amusement Parks	Dances
Parks, recreation centers	

Favorite Settings and Contexts, Ages 13 Through 15: Females

School	Video arcades
School events	Parks, recreation centers
Concert halls/amphitheaters	Convenience stores
Beaches	Music/video stores
Raves/Party scene	Street carnivals
Movie theaters	Home entertainment
Friends' houses	Ocean/underwater settings
Sporting events	Malls
Dances	Dining-out locations
Hiking/Mountains	
Shopping	

AGES 16 THROUGH 19

The 16-through-19-year-old is for all practical purposes fast becoming and behaving like a young adult. His "play" activities, preferred characters and settings/themes also reflect this coming of age. There are, however, remnant influences of childhood and certainly of early adolescence reflected in the 16-through-19-year-old's preferences. Males 16 through 19 do differ from their female counterparts in certain respects, but are more similar in their interests than at earlier stages of development.

Favorite Activities, Ages 16 Through 19: Males

Electronic games

Martial arts

Dining out

Entertaining at home

Watching TV/Videos

Going to movies

"Hanging out"

Surfing

Camping/Hiking

Dancing/going out dancing

Reading magazines

Reading books

Auto mechanics

Social clubs

Amusement parks

Music lessons/playing

Photography/video recording

Sports participation as players and as fans

Sci-Fi

Playing cards

Listening to radio

Listening to music

Going shopping

Internet/e-mail (computer communication)

Adult board games

Rollerblading

Concerts

Graphics, design, drawing, painting, sculpture

Using computers

Tools, woodworking

Seasonal sports: skiing, swimming

Getting/Sending mail

Favorite Activities, Ages 16 Through 19: Females

Going to movies

Dining out

Dancing/going out dancing

Shopping

Ceramics, sculpture, painting

Sports participation, watching

Roller skating, blading

Pets

Malls

Social clubs

Electronic games

Concerts

Amusement parks

Beach

Getting/sending mail

Board games

Watching TV/videos

Playing cards

Friends, socializing

Gymnastics

"Hanging out"

Swimming

Going to exhibits, fairs, museums

Horseback riding

Nature/ecology

Design, drawing, graphics

Listening to radio

Listening to music

Aerobics, fitness

Beginning college activities

Internet/e-mail (computer communication)

Character Identification, 16 Through 19: Males

Male sports celebrities	TV stars
Movie stars	Political figures
News commentators	Music celebrities
Religious/spiritual teachers	Race-car drivers
Action heroes	Talk-show hosts
Comedians	Parents
Teachers	Coaches
Female "bombshells"	Cartoon characters with "edge"— irreverent, dark-side, unique, rebellious

Character Identification, 16 Through 19: Females

Sports celebrities (male and female)	Comedians
Movie stars	"Hunks" (attractive males)
Soap-opera stars	TV Celebrities
Cartoon characters (with less "edge")	Talk-show hosts
Strong females in leadership positions	News commentators
Teachers	Religious/spiritual teachers
Parents	Political figures
Music celebrities	Models

Favorite Settings and Contexts, Ages 16 Through 19: Males

Sporting events	Pool/Billiard locations
Colleges and universities	Concerts/Amphitheaters
High schools	Malls
Friends' houses	Dining-out locations
Urban parks, basketball courts	Movie theaters
Beaches	Convenience stores
Mountains	Fairs, exhibitions, museums
Auto racetracks	Music/video stores
Party scenes	Travel destinations
Amusement parks	Dances
Parks, recreation centers	

Favorite Settings and Contexts, Ages 16 Through 19: Females

Colleges and universities	Dining-out locations
High school	Sporting events
Concert halls/amphitheaters	Parks, recreation centers
Beaches	Convenience stores
Party scene	Music/video stores
Movie theaters	Fairs, exhibitions, museums
Friends' houses	Home environments
Shopping locales	School events
Dances	Malls
Mountains	

GENDER AND MANUFACTURING/ PROGRAMMING CATEGORIES

Now that we've established and illustrated key differences between girls and boys as they progress through their developmental stages, let's look at the different manufacturing and programming efforts targeted at males and females, category by category.

TOYS AND TRADITIONAL GAMES: As can be discerned from this chapter's listings of favorite play activities, the toy and game preferences of males and females vary greatly. While these preferences change slightly from developmental stage to developmental stage, boys prefer action figures while girls prefer doll play. In general (and we must go out of our way to note that there *are* exceptions), boys prefer such activities as vehicle play (cars, trucks), electronic games, and construction play, whereas girls prefer playing such things as house, dress up, makeup play, and craft activities.

There *are* areas of common ground. For example when McDonald's or Burger King or Taco Bell comes out with a lineup of toys based on the latest Disney or Warner Brothers or other popular kid-targeted movie, both boys and girls 3 through 6 years old are attracted to *Lion King* or *Aladdin* or *Toy Story* toys. However, within the "cast" of characters and toys boys will prefer certain more male-appealing toys, e.g., villains, male heroes, whereas girls will prefer more female-appealing ones, e.g., female lead characters such as Pocahontas and "softer" animal characters. Then there are those films that are gender-biased, such as *Batman;* the toys from these skew quite male in their appeal.

Many traditional board and card games such as Hi-Ho! Cherry-O, Chutes and Ladders, Monopoly, UNO, Crazy Eights, and Scrabble are preferred by both sexes relatively equally, while other games are gender-biased. In the last decade or so, for example, Western Publishing Company and Milton Bradley have come out with communication- and relationships-oriented board games targeted at girls, games such as Girl Talk and Dream Phone. Strategic games such as chess and aggressively themed games like *Battleship* more often than not hold greatest appeal for boys.

The bottom line is that most toys and games are quite gender-biased. This is not to say, however, that toy-and-games companies should stop seeking products which contain themes, features, and processes that have dual gender appeal because history has taught us that these products occur over time. A technological innovation that arrived on the toy scene in the 1980s—the animatronic, talking, story-telling bear *Teddy Ruxpin*—is a good example of this dual gender appeal.

Whether we like it or don't, it is also true that while girls will often be comfortable with toys and games with predominantly male characters and themes (e.g., *Aladdin* toys and games), the reverse is seldom true; boys will seldom be comfortable with concepts with predominantly female lead characters and female themes, such as *Wonder Woman*. As far as we can tell, the reasons for this trace back to genetic and cultural differences formed over thousands of years, and appear to point to the fact that until recent times we Westerners have historically been patriarchal in our approaches to organizing ourselves socially.

As for trying to force square pegs into round holes by going against the grain of male and female preferences—whether innately caused or learned—toy and game manufacturers would be well advised to consider and thoroughly test whether there is truly an opportunity here or not. Although we must be careful not to make generalizations such as "girl action figures will never work"—witness the success of the *Power Rangers'* female action figures—there are certain generalizations that appear to stand up over time, such as "fashion dolls for boys will never work." It's hard to imagine a time when they might.

ELECTRONIC GAMES: As for traditional toys and games, there is a definite gender split in the kinds of games that appeal to boys and girls. There *are* games that reach common gender ground, such as "softer," less aggressive games like Mario Brothers, Pac-Man, and Zelda; role-playing games (even as sophisticated as *Myst*); and many games based on relatively "soft" Disney and Warner Brothers characters. The majority of games, however, both in the dedicated system arena (e.g., Nintendo, Sega, Sony Play Station) and the computer game arena, are male-biased in theme and content—fighting games such as Doom and Street Fighter, racing games such as Grand Prix Racing, and sports games such as NBA Jam. As we have said, statistics show that while approximately 20 percent of the overall game-playing audience is female, indications are also that a sizable number of the games that these girls are playing were purchased for someone else—a male in the family.

From a business standpoint, nonetheless, 20 percent is a large enough number to indicate definite interest and involvement on the part of females. Electronic game and computer companies would do well to continue to seek ways to create games with dual gender appeal and female-biased appeal. The more female-appropriate software succeeds in the marketplace, the more female appeal there will be.

TECHNOLOGICAL PRODUCTS: While there are many (especially utilitarian) technological products, such as electronic address books, calculators, and pocket flashlights that have relatively dual gender appeal, males—with their established propensities for things mechanical—tend to gravitate more than females toward technological innovations in the form of gadgets, gizmos, and the latest technological inventions.

SPORTS ITEMS: While obviously there are sports arenas that are quite male-biased, such as football, baseball, and boxing, and female-biased ones such as gymnastics and dance, most sports have strong appeal for both sexes.

APPAREL AND ACCESSORIES: Few surprises here. Males dress like males; females dress like females and males. Females do, however, starting at approximately age 7, demonstrate substantially more interest in and spend substantially more money on apparel and accessories than males. There are certain items of apparel, however, that receive a great deal of attention by both males and females. The proliferation of sneakers is a case in point. Having the right kind, the right brand of sneakers has become very important, even critical, to many children beginning at around age 7 and continuing through the teen years. What parent would have imagined ten years ago that she would be shelling out $120 for her fifth-grader's sneakers?

BRAND LOYALTY: It's interesting and important to note that brand loyalties often are formed quite early and may tend to last throughout a child's life. Surveys have shown, for example, that many young adults use the same brand of lipstick or cosmetics that they started with as a teenager. Some indications are that in certain product categories, brand loyalty can be as high as 80 percent as children mature into adulthood. Considering the tremendous monetary impact this figure implies, it's a mystery why more major corporations don't pay more attention to building brand loyalty from the earliest possible years. At YMS we have paid particular attention to the building of brand awareness and loyalty and have devised whole approaches designed to maximize this possibility.

PUBLICATIONS: Up until approximately the age of 5 or 6, kid-targeted publications such as *Disney Adventures* magazine are relatively unisex in their appeal. Most reading, however, occurs after this age and most publications take on distinct gender biasing. An examination of the findings of the 1996 Roper Youth Report, Table 9.1, clearly reveals these differences.

Table 9.1: Magazine Net Readership (13–17)

44.	Now, let's talk about magazines. Please look at the magazines on this list, and tell me which ones you read regularly, that is, more than half the issues published. Just call off the letters.
45.	And which ones do you read occasionally, that is, less than half the issues published?
46.	Now, please tell me which of these you subscribe to, that is, you receive it at home?

Boys	1996 Total %	1995 Total %	Girls	1996 Total %	1995 Total %
Sports Illustrated	40	40	Seventeen	50	52
TV Guide	19	25	Teen	38	38
National Geographic	15	14	YM (Young & Modern)	34	30
Game Players (Sega, Nintendo)	12	18	TV Guide	20	21
Mad Magazine	12	10	People	19	18
People	9	8	Cosmopolitan	15	22
Car & Driver	9	13	Glamour	14	21
Boys' Life	9	5	Ebony	13	10
Newsweek	9	9	Sassy	13	19
GamePro	8	11	Vogue	11	11

Note: Net readership is a combination of responses by students who either subscribe to or read a magazine title occasionally (less than half of issues published) or regularly. Chart represents the top ten answers out of 34 asked about.
© 1996 *Roper Youth Report,* Roper Starch Worldwide, 205 East 42nd Street, New York, NY 10017.

COMPUTER-LEARNING PROGRAMMING: Most computer-learning programming either is dual-gender–constructed to begin with or capitalizes on the fact that most girls tend to be comfortable with boy-themed content and characters in learning-software programming. Manufacturers need to be aware of the identification patterns of their target audience and the types and age-appropriateness of the characters utilized. Characters that are too soft, for example, may turn boys off, whereas too aggressive or otherwise "edgy" characters may turn girls away.

INTERNET PROGRAMMING: Programming utilizing the Internet, via both broad-based-interest and special-interest web sites, will also be divided into web sites with more female appeal and those with more male appeal. In general, girls will tend to seek out—beyond news and entertainment information that is dual-gender in its appeal—communications-based Internet activity and content, such as chat rooms and relationships-based information. They will also tend to use the Internet for shopping for items that appeal to them. Males will also be interested in generic news, shopping for male-appealing items, and entertainment information, but will have much stronger interest than girls in certain content such as sports news, financial and business matters, and science and technology.

FOOD AND BEVERAGES: No real differences here. Boys eat and girls eat, period. Boys in general do eat in greater quantities, however. Anyone with both boys and girls at home knows this at first hand. Food and beverage marketing efforts, however, need to be very sensitive to gender appeal. The wrong approach to packaging or TV ads or promotions could lead to gender biasing.

RESTAURANTS AND FAST-FOOD ESTABLISHMENTS: Again, there is not much difference in the types of restaurants and fast-food establishments that boys and girls tend to prefer and frequent. One arena in which caution must be taken, however, is promotions. A *Batman* movie tie-in for a fast-food chain, for example, won't have much of appeal for girls. Conversely, a *Pocahontas* tie-in will not have as much appeal for boys as, say, *Aladdin*.

TV PROGRAMMING: Kid-targeted and whole-family-targeted TV programming that contains content and characters which are more aggressive and/or "edgy" (controversial, rebellious, dark-sided), such as the Power Rangers or the Simpsons, is going to be more appealing to boys and less so to girls. Programs that stress relationship issues and that are less aggressive in their content, such as *Full House, Family Matters,* and *Saved by the Bell,* may be somewhat more popular with girls than with boys. Then there are those that find common ground, such as *Rugrats, Doug, Martin, Fresh Prince of Bel Air,* and *Home Improvement.*

FEATURE FILMS/HOME VIDEO: Feature films exhibited in theaters and later released for home video viewing—or films marketed direct to home video—not surprisingly share the same gender-biasing characteristics as TV programming. There are those films which are definitely male in their appeal, such as the latest Arnold Schwarzenegger, Bruce Willis, Sylvester Stallone, or Jean-Claude Van Damme action movie. Then there are those which are "girls'" or "women's" movies, such as *Waiting to Exhale.* And finally there are those which have mostly dual-gender appeal, such as *Home Alone, Forrest Gump,* or the latest Jim Carrey comedy.

MARKETING AND GENDER

Covered to a great extent in Chapter 11 on Successful Marketing to Kids, the same gender-biasing tendencies that occur in product and program appeal, as detailed above, occur when it comes to marketing. Whether attempting to market and advertise through packaging, TV advertising, radio, the Internet, publications, or promotions, certain generalizations apply.

1. For strictly female products and programs, we should take a strictly female-biased approach to marketing.
2. For strictly male products and programs, we should take a male-biased tack.
3. For those products and programs which are dual-gender targeted, we need to be careful to include elements of appeal to both sexes without turning off one or the other gender. As a general rule, females are more comfortable with marketing approaches featuring males as primary visuals, e.g., a male animal or human, real-life or animated, as a character prominently displayed on packaging, whereas males are not comfortable with marketing approaches featuring female characters as primary visuals.

SUMMARY

Whether the reader is a maximalist or a minimalist, and whether by nature or nurture, genuine and definitive differences *do* exist between young boys and girls as they mature and work their way through the successive developmental stages into adulthood. A product developer or marketer would have his or her head buried in the sand if failing to recognize these differences. However, some rules are made to be broken and generalizations often fall apart in the face of innovation. Realistic planning and innovative thinking, as well as continued research and development, is the order of the day when we dare to strap on our battle gear and enter the battlefields of the gender wars.

CHAPTER 10

KIDS AND CHARACTERS

"Ehh . . . What's up, Doc?" —Bugs Bunny
"I tawt I taw a puddy tat." —Tweety Bird
"Holy cow, Man!" —Bart Simpson
"@&*#@#%!!" —Tasmanian Devil

It's hard to imagine what life would be like if it were not populated with characters—not only the fantasy Bugs Bunny and Garfield and Barbie®, not only the fantasy superhuman characters such as Batman and Superman, but also the human "characters" that we love to love, such as Sylvester Stallone's Rocky or Michael Jordan as a bigger-than-life superstar. And then there are those characters we love to hate, such as J.R. Ewing of *Dallas* in the 1980s, Darth Vader of the *Star Wars* movies, the latest soap-opera villains, or the Joker in the *Batman* stories.

As long as humans have been around, there have been characters. Classical Greek and Roman mythology sported a great variety of characters—characters to emulate, characters to fear, characters to entertain. Native American groups such as the Zuni and Hopi have all sorts of spirit characters, which are represented as wooden kachina dolls and which are a rich part of the cultural story and religious rituals of these peoples to this day—their people dress up in kachina costumes for ceremonial plays and dances. Earlier in the 20th century our "hero" characters were sports stars such as boxers, and the cowboys and outlaws, heroes and villains that were found in the pages of books and comics of the day.

Today the character population on this planet appears to be experiencing a birth rate equal to the human population at large. There are characters everywhere. Television is filled with cartoon mascots jumping up and down over cereals, toys, snacks, fast food, and sneakers. Our grocery shelves are jumping with cartoon animals and sports heroes of all kinds. Electronic games and "edutainment" software titles abound with characters. The Olympics are not without a new cartoon mascot every four years, and the stories on TV and in the movies are all about characters.

Kids of course have an enormous attraction to characters. In this chapter we put that attraction under a microscope to determine where this "character power" lies and what its dynamics are.

KIDS AND CHARACTERS: WHAT'S THE PAYOFF?

Beyond the obvious "fun" that characters deliver to kids, let's look at the underlying attraction that kids have to characters. In order to examine this phenomenon, we have to return to our discussion of Identification from Chapter 4. Kids essentially relate to or identify with characters in one of four ways.

A. NURTURING: The character either nurtures the child (like Barney) or is nurtured by the child (like a doll).

B. LIKE ME: The child identifies with the character as being like himself, or with some aspect or quality of the character as being like himself.

C. EMULATION: The child wants to be like the character in some way.

D. DISIDENTIFICATION: The child is attracted to the dark-side qualities of the character. He does not consciously want to be like the character—often a villain—but is "entertained" by his violent, negative, abusive, or otherwise evil ways.

What a child's payoff is or what he "gets out of" his relationship with a character or characters is that he gets his needs met in some regard. If a character such as Big Bird is a nurturing character, a 4-year-old can feel love and safety from him. If Barbie® represents success to a 6-year-old girl, than this 6-year-old can emulate this success and experience it vicariously through Barbie as a role model. If The Joker and other *Batman* villains such as The Penguin display their evil treachery—expressing the darker sides of humanity that I am not allowed to openly express—and if I am an 8-year-old boy, I can find it very entertaining without having to behave that way myself, and in fact I can enjoy the villain's deserved demise.

This same child also may not particularly identify with a given character but may just find him very colorful and animated or funny and therefore very entertaining. Put a fruit snack targeted to 3-through-7-year-olds in a plain box with the name FRUIT SNACK on it and place beside it the same snack in the same box but with a goofy shark character on the front of the box and it will be a surprise to no one which box the 3-through-7-year-old will pick 95 times out of a hundred: the one with the character.

Why? Because a fruit snack or any other object inside a box is only one part of the "product" that the child is attracted to; he is attracted to the entire "gestalt"; everything he sees and hears has potential payoff for him—so much so that many times the product is almost incidental. What the child is most interested in, at least at first, is the premium inside the box, or looking at a fun character, or doing the maze on the package back.

Think of it as a series of events. From a below-7-year-old's point of view, the first "event" of a McDonald's Happy Meal is the characters on the Happy Meal box along with the colorful graphics and maybe a maze or a game to play or jokes and riddles to read. Then the next "event" is the toy or other premium inside the box, and finally—oh by the way—there's the "event" of the hamburger itself. Adults are not like this. Adults are attracted like anyone else to attractive graphics and colors on packaging and will respond to a product well named, but their primary focus is on what's inside the box and what it is going to deliver.

Characters bring enormous attraction and involvement to kid-targeted advertising as well. Licensed characters such as the Animaniacs, with their wild and crazy antics on TV ads for Life cereal, will get far more attention than the cereal itself.

THE MANUFACTURER'S PAYOFF

From a product manufacturer's point of view, there is also much to gain from utilizing characters. Beyond the obvious attraction to the package and product that they supply, characters also bring two advantages.

A. EQUITY: They become an "equity" unto themselves, since the child finds them as rewarding as, or more rewarding than, the product itself in many cases.

B. COMPETITIVE EDGE: Whereas competitors can easily reproduce a similar product, they may find it difficult to compete with a manufacturer's strong and effective proprietary or licensed character. Tony the Tiger and Kellogg's Frosted Flakes, for example, are almost synonymous. They have been mentally "linked" by appearing together on the shelves and in advertising so much over the years.

WINNING CHARACTERS

What is it that the most popular characters of all time have that other, weaker characters do not have? What is it about Bugs Bunny, who after so many years still remains at the top of the charts in popularity? And isn't it interesting that in a cartoon head-to-head competition, Bugs is more attractive and involving to more Americans, across a wider age range, than Mickey Mouse? Why is that? What is it about Barbie® that turns a billion-plus dollars at the cash registers year after year? What does Tasmanian Devil have that other characters lack?

GARFIELD

Let's put Garfield, one of the strongest and most effective characters of all time, under the microscope to determine what gives him such power.

At the Character Lab, a division of Youth Market Systems Consulting, we have devised two key "tools" to assist us both in getting at the underlying power dynamics of a given character and to design powerful and effective characters from scratch. The first of these tools is the Character Appeal Quadrant Analysis form. Let's look at Garfield's Character Appeal Quadrant Analysis form, which is on page 163. Then we'll discuss it.

The Character Appeal Quadrant Analysis is designed to get at a character's "power" with the intended audience. If you'll notice, only the lower left "quadrant" of this model contains characteristics/traits that are "Low" in power. The right side of the model, that is the upper right and lower right quadrants, contains those traits that are the most powerful. As you can easily see, Garfield sports the majority of these strong and powerful characteristics. In fact, more than most other effective characters, he manifests many of these traits, such as Impulsiveness, Meanness, and Manipulation, to the Nth degree.

If we contrasted with Garfield less-powerful characters such as Elmer Fudd or Tweety Bird or Minnie Mouse and if we "charted" their characteristics using the Character Appeal Quadrant Analysis, we'd find that they manifest far-less-powerful traits. Although it's perhaps unfair to compare characters that are designed and intended to represent different types of traits and archetypes, the comparison is useful to learn from nevertheless.

CHARACTER PERSONALITY

When evaluating the relative power and effectiveness of a character, or when designing a character from scratch, it's very important to be able to see the character's whole "personality," or the component parts that he or she is made of, as much as this is possible.

Table 10.1: Character Appeal Quadrant Analysis

Character   Garfield

POWER

	HIGH			HIGH	
I	NO	Light-side character	YES		Unique/Different
D	NO	Vulnerable	YES		Hero/Winner archetype
E	NO	Tender	YES		Intelligent/Clever
N	NO	Innocent*	YES		A Leader
T	NO	Loving	YES		Happy/Carefree
I	NO	Shy	YES		Independent
F			NO		Warm/Friendly*
Y			YES		Multidimensional
			YES		Funny/Humorous
			YES		Exciting/Stimulating
			YES		Competitive
			NO		Nurturing
			YES		Self-assured/Confident
			YES		Physically appealing
			YES		Emotionally expressive
D	NO	Non-unique, Passé	YES		Darkside character
I	NO	Loser archetype	YES		Mean
S	NO	Dupe/Stupid	YES		Manipulative
I	NO	Follower	YES		Moody/Anxious
D	NO	Dependent	YES		Abusive
E	NO	Unidimensional	YES		Obnoxious
N	NO	No humor	YES		Impulsive
T	NO	Predictable	YES		Rebellious
I	NO	Boring/unemotional			
F	NO	Non-unique			
Y	NO	Physically unappealing			
	LOW			HIGH	

*Only if he's manipulating someone
© YMS™/Character Lab/The Center for Innertainment®

BUGS BUNNY'S CHARACTER SUMMARY

In addition to the above Character Appeal Quadrant Analysis, a second character-lab research tool is the Character Summary that follows (see page 164), this time using Bugs Bunny as an example.

CHARACTER SUMMARY

CHARACTER NAME: __BUGS BUNNY__

GENDER: __✓__ F __ M FEMALENESS 1 2 3 ④ 5 MALENESS

DEVELOPMENTAL STAGE: __Teen-adult__

ANIMAL/HUMAN: __Rabbit__

SOMATOTYPE (BODY TYPE): __Mesomorph__

NEEDS: __Needs little - self-sufficient__

WANTS/AFFINITIES: __Carrots, taking it easy, overcoming__
__adversaries through outsmarting them__

PREDOMINANT BEHAVIORS: __Outsmarting antagonists,__
__eating carrots__

BEHAVIOR RANGE: __Wide__

PREDOMINANT EMOTIONS: __Calm, cool, confident__

EMOTIONAL RANGE: __Moderate__

ENERGY LEVEL: ___ Low __X__ Medium ___ High ___ Very High

CONTROL STYLE:

__X__ PHYSICAL	___ NURTURING
__X__ INTELLECTUAL	___ COOPERATIVE
___ SOCIAL	__X__ COMPETITIVE
__X__ EMOTIONAL	__X__ MANIPULATIVE
___ ETHICAL	___ ABUSIVE

CONTROL RANGE: __Broad/very effective__

KEY RELATIONSHIPS:
1. Porky Pig
2. Elmer Fudd   Antagonist
3. Yosemite Sam   Antagonist
4. Daffy Duck

MARKETABLE QUALITIES: __Cute, clever/smart,__
__affinity for carrots, Easter__

CHARACTER ATTITUDE: __Happy-go-lucky__

CHARACTER'S "PHILOSOPHY OF LIFE"/MISSION

Life is about: __Being happy and outsmarting/foiling any__
__would-be antagonists__

LANGUAGE ELEMENTS/IDIOSYNCRASIES: __Characteristic voice__

QUOTABLES: __"What's up, Doc?"__

HUMOR STYLE:

__X__ PHYSICAL SLAPSTICK Causes it to happen to others

__X__ SUDDEN SURPRISE/THE UNEXPECTED/THE TABOO

__X__ INCONGRUITY/IRRATIONALITY

__X__ AFFECTIONATE RIDICULE/SARCASM/"SUDDEN SUPERIORITY"

__X__ VICTIM/BUTT OF JOKE/FALL GUY

__X__ RECKLESS ABANDON

__X__ GAGS/JOKES/PUNS/WISECRACKS

__X__ SATIRE

___ WORD PLAY

__X__ SPEECH/LANGUAGE ELEMENTS Characteristic voice

___ OTHER

CHARACTER ARCHETYPE/ROLE

__X__ LIGHT-SIDE CHILD __X__ DARK-SIDE CHILD __X__ HERO

___ HEROINE   ___ FATHER   ___ WISE OLD MAN

___ MOTHER   ___ WISE OLD WOMAN ___ SIDEKICK

__X__ JESTER   ___ VILLAIN   ___ WITCH

___ VICTIM   ___ BUFFOON   ___ UNDERDOG

ESSENCE OF CHARACTER: __Cute & clever winner rabbit__

Some of the aspects of the Character Summary may need elaboration or clarification:

FEMALENESS/MALENESS: Even though a given character is male, his degree of maleness or "machismo" will differ from other male characters. The same for female characters. They also will differ in their degree of femininity. Some characters like Tweety Bird, for example, are relatively asexual. While he's a boy, he's so innocent and cute (except when he's cunningly laying a trap for Sylvester) that he appears almost female. Or, if I could put my tongue in my cheek for a moment, as some psychologists might say, maybe Tweety Bird has matured sufficiently to be comfortable with his "feminine side."

DEVELOPMENTAL STAGE: This term refers to which age/stage the character is in: the 0-through-2 infant/toddler stage, the 3-through-7 early-childhood stage, the 8-through-12 Rule/Role stage, the 13-through-15 early-adolescent stage, the 16-through-19 late-adolescent stage, or one of the several adult developmental stages.

SOMATOTYPE: It's useful to know which body type the character has. There are essentially three somatotypes: the endomorph or soft and chubby, the mesomorph or muscular with a medium build, and the ectomorph, which is a thin, wiry body type.

NEEDS: At the Character Lab we have identified ten basic needs of human beings: Physical Needs, Safety, Growth, Love, Acceptance, Success, Stimulation, Control, Reality, and Release. Typically, the less a character needs the more powerful he is; conversely the more needy or dependent a character is, the less power he has. (True for humans also, by the way.)

BEHAVIOR RANGE: A character's range of behavior may vary greatly. For example, Road Runner has quite a narrow range of behavior. He essentially speeds around on dirt roads, eats seeds, and fortuitously avoids Wile E. Coyote's traps. Wile E. Coyote, on the other hand, displays a wide range of behaviors as he designs and carries out his schemes.

ENERGY LEVEL: A character's "energy level" refers primarily to his activity level. Is he very animated, for example, always in a frenzy like Tasmanian Devil? Or is he lethargic like Eeyore of Winnie the Pooh fame? Or is he somewhere in between? This is an important determination and should be linked to the "essence" of the product or program and what is trying to be accomplished.

CONTROL STYLE: This refers to the way in which the character controls or dominates other characters. In essence, a character uses certain of his faculties—his physical body (strength) or an extension of his body such as a weapon, his mind or smarts, his social status, his emotions, or his moral righteousness—to control others. And the way in which he uses these faculties can be in a nurturing manner or it can be cooperative, competitive, manipulative, or abusive.

KEY RELATIONSHIPS/CHARACTER DYNAMIC: At the Character Lab we always take into account the possibility of the increased power that can be attained by the use of a central character in a dynamic relationship with another character or characters. What is the Road Runner's power without the story/conflict of having Wile E. Coyote lurking nearby? Who is Batman without The Joker? Tweety Bird without Sylvester the Cat? Who is Garfield without Odie or his owner Jon to abuse? Bugs Bunny without Elmer Fudd and his shotgun? Or who is Mickey Mouse without Minnie? Characters in relationship with one another bring romance and friendship and story and drama and conflict to a product or program. On a package front, for example, our recommendation is, whenever possible, and when the characters' makeup allows, to present characters in relationship with each other, e.g., Batman as the central figure with The Joker threatening in some way as a secondary visual image.

CHARACTER'S "PHILOSOPHY OF LIFE"/MISSION: In most cases, it is very important to clearly define a character's "philosophy of life" and "mission." What is he up to? Whether it's Batman, whose mission is to protect and serve Gotham City, or Wile E. Coyote, whose "philosophy of life" might be summarized as "Never give up" and whose mission is to "catch that rascal Road Runner," a clearly articulated philosophy/mission guides the character's actions and provides program developers, writers, marketers, and advertisers with directions and guidelines that have continuity.

LANGUAGE ELEMENTS/IDIOSYNCRASIES: This refers to language quirks or attributes a character might have, such as Elmer Fudd's stuttering, or a character might talk baby talk, repeat himself all the time, etc. "Idiosyncrasies" are typically behavioral characteristics such as a nervous twitch or a habit of brushing back their hair or always eating lots of hot dogs or wearing strange hats. These language-based and behavioral "signatures" add humor and dimension to characters and make them more attractive and involving.

QUOTABLES: Relatively self-explanatory, "quotables" are those signature phrases that we come to know characters by. Bugs's "What's up, Doc?" has served him well for many years. Then there's Porky Pig's famous "Uh, bedeuh bedeuh, that's all folks!" and Fred Flintstone's "Yabba dabba doo!" and Jackie Gleason's "One a these days Alice, Bam! to the moon!" and the Lone Ranger's "Hi-yo Silver! Away!"

HUMOR STYLE: It's very critical to be aware of the types of humor that are delivered by a given character—especially with a child target in mind. Since understanding of, and therefore the entertainment value of, certain sophisticated kinds of humor such as innuendo, puns, plays on words, and sarcasm depends on sufficient cognitive development, to utilize excessive degrees of this advanced humor while targeting very young children is a mistake. Many successful programs and humorous concepts do what we call "layering" of humor in that on one level, perhaps a visual level, very visual slapstick humor is utilized that has appeal to younger as well as older audiences, while at the same time on a verbal level more sophisticated humor is used that stretches the character's appeal upward through the teen years and to adults. Bugs Bunny's success is exemplary in its effectiveness using this type of layering.

CHARACTER ARCHETYPE: Perhaps no other aspect of a character is more important to establish and be certain about than his "archetype." "Archetypes" are basic character types that have been utilized down through the centuries and that have proven effective in capturing and illustrating different human personality types, roles, and relationships. When designing a character from scratch or redesigning one, or when simply attempting to maximize the use and deployment of a character or characters, it is critical to know what that character's archetype/role or roles are and how those roles interrelate with other characters and their archetypes/roles. In Bugs Bunny's Character Summary, for example, note that his archetypes/roles are split between "light and dark-side child," "hero," and "jester."

ESSENCE OF CHARACTER: It is also very helpful in terms of providing continuity and guidance for a character's Essence to be clearly established and supported by all the parties that utilize a given character. The term "Essence" as it is used here refers to the concise summing up of a character's personality, archetype, role in as few words as possible. The Tasmanian Devil character, for example, might be "essenced" as: "Wild-eyed and frenzied, eat-everything-in-sight whirling dervish Tasmanian Devil."

DEVELOPMENTAL STAGES AND CHARACTERS

While we have utilized character likes and dislikes and preferences throughout this book's chapters on the succeeding age segments, it would be enlightening to revisit each of the age segments and discuss characters in relationship to these different developmental stages.

AGES BIRTH THROUGH 2

Mothers, as "gatekeepers" and protectors of their young, instinctively choose primarily soft and safe characters for their infants and toddlers— characters such as generic kitties, puppies, rabbits and bears, and licensed characters such as Barney or Big Bird or Mickey Mouse and his friends. Putting them under the microscope, we would easily see that these young-appealing characters share many physical and personality characteristics with their baby buddies. They are typically round and have round heads, ears, and bodies; they typically have or show no teeth, usually sporting only gums; and they have friendly, pleasant personalities. Edgier characters such as Tasmanian Devil and Garfield are avoided for the most part by parents of the very young in favor of characters with very soft and safe qualities.

AGES 3 THROUGH 7

For the purpose of character selection and utilization for this particular age spread, it would be important to think of the 3-through-7-year-old stage as two distinct stages. For the younger end of this stage, 3-through-5-year-olds, preferred characters by both parents and kids themselves are still relatively soft and safe. Most any of the popular Disney characters (e.g., Mickey Mouse, Minnie, Goofy, Donald Duck) and the Warner Brothers Looney Tunes line-up of characters (Bugs Bunny, Daffy Duck, Tweety Bird and Sylvester, Elmer Fudd, Tasmanian Devil) are appropriate and effective for this younger stage—with the exception of perhaps Tasmanian Devil, if he's baring too many teeth and acting too scary for a 3- or 4-year-old.

By the time the child has entered into the older end of this 3-through-7 stage, i.e., by ages 6 and 7, he is more sophisticated in his character preferences and will want or require characters with more complexities and more edge, that is, more sophisticated humor and dark-side behaviors and personality traits. Barney's appeal will not only be diminished by this time; children will sometimes need to aggressively "push away" from these youngish characters as a sort of rite of passage as they mature into the 7+ years. Now children will start to prefer characters like Wile E. Coyote, Bugs Bunny with his sophisticated humor style, Garfield, Tasmanian Devil's aggressiveness, and the Animaniacs' wild antics. As a generalization throughout this stage, boys will tend to prefer the more aggressive characters and girls will tend to prefer softer, less aggressive characters.

AGES 8 THROUGH 12

Not only because of the cognitive maturation that has taken place by this period of development, (i.e., the development of the left hemisphere of the brain), but also because of social maturation, children throughout the 8-through-12 stage will want more complicated, more sophisticated, edgier characters. It is very important to note that there is a distinct difference now in the types of characters that most appeal to boys and to girls. Boys move rapidly into preference for very edgy and sometimes aggressive characters such as the Animaniacs, Tasmanian Devil, and Garfield, as well as very aggressive characters such as Marvel's X-Men and other comic-book characters. Meanwhile girls, while they may enjoy the antics of the Animaniacs or Garfield or Road Runner and Wile E. Coyote, they will also tend to prefer softer, more feminine characters such as Tweety Bird, puppies and kitties and such, the latest Disney feature-film characters such as those from *Beauty and the Beast, Aladdin,* or *Hercules,* and of course, Barbie®. Both males and females begin to identify with real-life characters during these years as well—the Wayne Gretzkys and Bruce Willises and Madonnas of the world.

AGES 13+

By the time children reach adolescence, their taste in characters has matured to the point that they have moved away from most of the cartoonish characters that have very young appeal and toward more human characters such as sports celebrities, music celebs such as Madonna, human movie and TV stars, and human fantasy stars like Batman, Luke Skywalker, and the *Star Trek* characters. The one exception is that late teens as well as adults respond positively to nostalgic mainstream culture characters such as

Mickey Mouse or Bugs Bunny or Garfield when presented in certain formats, e.g., on apparel, calendars, joke books, coffee mugs, and other household or office accessories. Many adults have elaborate collections built around these characters.

LICENSING CHARACTERS

Many companies utilize the powerful equity that popular characters have to great advantage by licensing them for use with their product lineup—or *as* their products, in the case of toy characters. Fast-food companies are constantly offering premiums tied in to the latest Disney or Warner Brothers feature film releases such as *Aladdin* or *Hercules* or the latest *Batman*. Packaged-goods companies such as cereal companies, kid-targeted snack companies, and beverage companies also use licensed characters to great advantage.

While strategic deployment of a popular character or cast of characters under a licensing program can be very effective, there are four definite pitfalls to watch out for.

A. OUTDATED CHARACTERS: While it is true that certain characters might be less expensive to license because they are a bit outdated, don't expect them to perform as well as more up-to-date characters. Children can quickly change their "filters" or "frames of reference" for what's hot and what's not and you need to stay on top of current character favorites. As a licensee, you get what you pay for; this should not be overlooked.

B. TARGET AGE MISMATCH: One of the biggest problems that companies who license characters encounter is that they miscalculate the appeal or lack of appeal of a given character or set of characters for their intended kid-consumer target. Disney characters as a whole, for example, because of their softer, less aggressive makeup, skew younger for many categories such as supermarket foods, fast foods, and kid-targeted apparel. Warner Brothers characters, on the other hand, because of their darker, more aggressive qualities, skew slightly older. Each character or set of characters should be considered and even tested carefully to ensure maximum age appropriateness and appeal for a company's intended target consumer group.

C. GENDER BIAS: Some companies tie their product in to characters without carefully considering how females, for example, might respond quite differently to the characters than males. Marvel's X-

Men, for example, are going to be more appealing to males, whereas The Littlest Mermaid is going to be female-biased. Garfield and Tasmanian Devil, because of their edgy, aggressive personalities and behaviors, may be slightly more male-biased. Real-life sports stars such as John Elway or Michael Jordan, or Mike Piazza of the L.A. Dodgers, are going to be more male-biased as well. Tweety Bird and Winnie the Pooh, although males, because of their "soft" and relatively "light-sided" personalities are going to skew female. Characters such as the Animaniacs and Bugs Bunny, on the other hand, are relatively gender-bias free.

D. WEAK DEPLOYMENT: Another "pitfall" of licensed character use is not utilizing the characters in an optimal manner. *Children are primarily visual in their orientation to stimuli.* Therefore when characters are utilized, whether licensed or proprietary to the company as the Trix Rabbit is to General Mills and the MooTown cow is to Sargento Cheese Co., they should be maximized on packaging, in advertising, and as premiums. Often adult minds—which are more verbal and logical than child minds—push for the product name or "brand" to be the primary visual on packaging or a too-prominent aspect of TV advertising. Given the visual mentality of kids, the most effective use of a character or characters is to make them the central visual on the package and in ads. The way that General Mills typically portrays the Trix Rabbit, for example, is that he takes up about two thirds of the front-panel real estate on the cereal box package. If kids are your primary target, this is an example of optimal deployment of a character.

When there is a character lineup that has a story as part of its equity, as in *101 Dalmatians,* for example, it is also advisable to "tell the story" visually in some way—especially in this case, through depicting the conflict between the Dalmatians and the story's villain, Cruella. Not to visually tell the story may be to miss an opportunity.

BUILDING PROPRIETARY CHARACTERS FROM SCRATCH

Given the enormous potential for appeal of a character or characters, it's no accident that there is a proliferation of characters in the kid-targeted marketplace as well as the adult marketplace. For adults, for example, witness the success of the Disney and Warner Brothers retail stores, in which a great deal of the purchasing is for adult use.

If I have a kid-targeting peanut-butter company or an apparel company or a fast-food chain, and I have no proprietary "character program," I would do well to consider developing one. What follows is a step-by-step How-To recipe for developing such a program.

A. KNOW YOUR TARGET: What is the age range that you are targeting? Is it 3 through 7? Is it 8 through 12? Is it 3 through 12? If it is as broad as 3 through 12 then you definitely have a challenge, because many times characters are either youngish in their appeal, like the Disney lineup, or older in their appeal, like Ren and Stimpy. Not so common are characters that have appeal across such a broad age range. There *are* such characters, however. Bugs Bunny is one such character, because through the "filter" that a 4-year-old uses he's a cute and attractive bunny rabbit with an entertaining voice and funny antics, while through an 11-year-old's "filter" he is an attractive and acerbic, sarcastic, cunning, manipulative, funny rabbit. And don't forget *gender*. You also need to consider the relative appeal of a character to males as opposed to females, or to both at once.

B. KNOW YOUR CATEGORY: If you are selling food that is going to be consumed outside the home (such as fast food), then the "billboard effect" is working—that is, kids over the age of approximately 6 or 7 are going to be aware of and concerned about what character or characters they are seen to be associated with. If the character is on a snack-food or cereal box that is going to be consumed in the safety of one's own home, then more youngish characters can be accepted by older kids. The same applies for apparel to a great degree, although because so many adults happily wear "young" licensed characters on their shirts, sweatshirts, socks, ties, etc., the stigma is removed or lessened in many cases. If you are a software manufacturer, it will be very critical what age-and-gender appeal any characters you may create and deploy might have. Children are very quick to make "for me" or "not for me" judgments when presented with a given character.

C. KNOW YOUR PRODUCT'S "ESSENCE": While it might be said that a tiger has little to do with the "essence" of frosted flakes, Tony the Tiger has obviously been very successful as a spokescharacter for Kellogg's. It is possible to create a powerful character and simply associate him with your product. In other cases, however, it is very desirable to create a character that captures the "essence" of your product. One of the pioneer characters with the longest longevity in the marketplace, for example, is Mr. Peanut. He says—he exemplifies—he *embodies* Planter's Peanuts.

At the Character Lab we were recently assigned by Kraft/Post Cereals of Canada the task of creating a "spokescharacter" for a new cereal named Fruity Crisps. True to its name, the cereal is crispy and very colorful with bright fruit colors. The character we designed, therefore, is a very colorfully dressed, *cool* crocodile with sunglasses and a green, red, and purple striped shirt.

Spending the time and energy to correctly "essence" your product and getting everyone's understanding and support for that essence— new-product development people, marketers, advertisers, and other product team members—is critical to the success of that product, including the development and maintenance of any character program you might wish to establish.

D. DEVELOP ALTERNATIVE APPROACHES: If you rely on only one creative direction, you may not see other alternatives that could turn out to be more effective. The recommendation is to create at least two or three alternative directions for your character. You may want to use different artists for these alternatives as well.

E. TEST ALTERNATIVE DIRECTIONS: The ideal is to thoroughly test the proposed character directions in order to get at their relative strength with your targeted consumers. Focus groups are the best starting point. Then, taking what you have learned from these groups, make revisions and move into a quantitative test phase, the results of which should provide sufficient certainty about your creative directions. Then improve, revise, and improve some more.

ANIMAL OR HUMAN?

One of the questions that almost always arises when a company is considering the development of a proprietary character for a kid-targeted product is "Should we develop an animal or human character?" As a general rule of thumb, below the age of 7 (that is before the child has entered into the 8-through-12 Rule/Role or more logical stage of development), animal characters are much more likely to have power than human characters. This is actually true in many cases for the 8-through-12 stage as well, but to a lesser extent. There are essentially two reasons for this popularity of animal characters over human ones. They are as follows.

THE USE OF ANIMALS AVOIDS "LIKE ME" ASSOCIATIONS: If you were to use a human character it would either be male and therefore not like females, or female and not like males. Children are very quick to make "for me" or "not for me" decisions, and if a character is "not like them" it can bring about rejection. A human character would also be perceived to be a particular age that is not likely to match the target's age. Animal characters, by contrast, are relatively asexual, as perceived by both boys and girls. For example, Winnie the Pooh is male, but because of his soft cuddly bear qualities he is cute and approachable by both sexes. Animal characters are also more ageless than humans. Children are quick to identify how old a human is, but are not as concerned with animal ages; and it's not easy to determine an animal's age, anyway.

THE CHILD–ANIMAL RELATIONSHIP: The first thing to note about the relationship that children have with animals is that it is, except for those animals that might frighten or threaten a child, a very intimate, loving relationship. Children easily enjoy both giving animals love and receiving love from them—especially the domestic animals, the cats, dogs, rabbits, hamsters, birds, and such with whom they share their space. This "nurture" and "be nurtured by" relationship is very strong, and of course lasts throughout people's lives. A little-known fact about children and animals that underscores this special relationship between them is that studies of children below the age of 6 and the content of their dreams reveal that as much as 90 percent of such children's dreams are of animals.

From cereal boxes to software to cartoons to children's literature to T-shirts, characters share this planet Earth with us, and in fact it would be hard to imagine a world without them. What would it be like to have no cartoon characters on TV? No Alf? No Garfield? No Bart Simpson? No Pink Panther? No Clark Kent and Lois Lane? What would the moviegoing experience be without Rocky and Darth Vader and 007 and Indiana Jones? Grocery shelves without characters colorfully populating package fronts? Hard to imagine.

Yet the creation, development, and utilization of a character or characters without careful consideration of the relationship that your targeted consumer will have with the character or characters you deploy leaves the outcome—the impact on sales and on repeat-purchase patterns—in question. What is needed is a well-thought-out "character program" that uses characters that are attractive, powerful, and—most of all—appropriate for the intended targets.

CHAPTER 11

SUCCESSFUL MARKETING
TO KIDS

$\int$uccessful marketing to kids means reaching kids. And in order to reach kids you have to go where kids are and know what mediums they pay attention to. The important thing to consider is that these change dramatically depending on which age children you are targeting. This chapter, therefore, is organized around each of the different age segments as presented in Chapters 4 through 8.

EFFECTIVENESS CRITERIA:
THE BASICS OF MARKETING TO KIDS

Successful marketing to kids also means appealing to them so that they are either motivated to purchase an item themselves or ask their parents to buy it for them; this is known as "purchase influence," or less formally as "the nag factor." Before diving into each of the age segments, let's lay some groundwork for understanding what needs to happen in order for a targeted child consumer to be effectively impacted through marketing strategies. At Youth Market Systems (YMS) Consulting we have for a number of years successfully utilized a model that we call the YMS Effectiveness Criteria Checklist.

We say that in order for a potential consumer to be sufficiently impacted, ideally we must accomplish taking them through a series of "steps." First they must *pay attention,* then they must *comprehend* what is being presented to them, then they must perceive enough payoff in the stimulus to *involve* them, then they must form a positive attitude toward wanting it, in essence *"yielding"* to it, then must be motivated to take the *action* of purchase or of requesting it, then once having it they must have a continued positive *reaction* to it, and finally and ideally they will *communicate* good things about it, even to the point of recommending it to others. Below is the YMS Effectiveness Criteria Checklist followed by an annotated Effectiveness Criteria Model.

The YMS Effectiveness Criteria Checklist

_____ Attention
_____ Comprehension
_____ Involvement
_____ Yield
_____ Action
_____ Reaction
_____ Communication

AN EFFECTIVENESS CRITERIA MODEL

Although these Effectiveness Criteria are presented as if they were sequential steps, they do not remain separate in all cases. For example, part of the reason why a potential kid consumer might pay attention (see Attention) to something is because as soon as he perceives the item, he immediately becomes involved (see Involvement) because it is something that promises him payoff or gratification. "Attention" and "Involvement" therefore are inextricably interrelated and for all practical purposes almost simultaneous.

ATTENTION: *To what degree does the concept "grab" the attention of its intended purchaser or user?* With all the competitive "clutter" in the media and in the marketplace, if you don't get the child's (or parent's) attention, you will not get to first base, so to speak.

COMPREHENSION: *How easy is the concept to understand?* Children, especially below the age of 7, are very visual in their approach to "getting" what is being presented to them. If what you present is highly visual and presented concretely rather than in a way that is too abstract, it is likely to be easily understood. This visual predominance holds true even after age 7, but in a more integrative way, because now we are dealing with a child who has the cognitive ability to be interested in more verbal content.

INVOLVEMENT: *How deeply engaged is the purchaser/user likely to become with the concept? What "payoff" does he perceive is "in it for him"? What needs does it meet?* Along with "Attention," this component of the Effectiveness Criteria is the most critical. Children, perhaps even more intensely than adults, get an immediate "hit" or "read" on what's in it for them when presented with any given stimulus. While strong communications via TV advertising or print ads, or on packaging, certainly will have a first-stage impact on children, what the product or program actually delivers in fun, play value, pleasure, taste, etc., will have the strongest effect—hopefully a lasting and repeat effect stimulating repeat interest in purchasing, having, and enjoying the item.

YIELD: *How intense is the targeted consumer's degree of positive attitude formation toward wanting to purchase or own the concept?* This is relatively self-explanatory. Attitude formation is obviously critical in that the goal is for the targeted consumer to form a strong and positive attitude toward wanting to have the item in question. It is very helpful, therefore, especially when comparing the child's degree of interest in competitive items, to be able to get a read on and qualitatively and/or quantitatively measure *the degree of, or lack of, interest or excitement targeted children have for your item.*

ACTION: *How likely is the target consumer to take the action of purchase?* Again this is quite self-explanatory. It is important, however, to understand at what ages children make direct purchases themselves and in what categories—versus those "influence" purchases that result from the child taking the action of making requests of his parents or grandparents.

REACTION: *After having used the product, what is the likely degree of satisfaction? How likely is the user to return to use it again and again?* As you can see here there are two aspects to Reaction. The first is how the child reacts *initially* to using or otherwise "consuming" the product or program. Then, there is the question of *ongoing satisfaction* such that the child is motivated to "re-act" or "act again" by wanting to use the product over and over again, assuming a nonconsumable item, or motivated to purchase another one, assuming a consumable item.

COMMUNICATION: *How likely is the purchaser/user to be so satisfied as to communicate about and recommend this product to others (positive word of mouth)?* There are several venues of communication implicit here. The first is *self-communication,* or what the child (or parent) is *saying to himself* regarding the product or program. Then, ideally, there will be such enthusiasm for it that the child spontaneously *communicates positively to others* about his satisfaction or enthusiasm for it, e.g., to his parents, his siblings, his friends. Finally, the most ideal outcome would be for the child or parent to *strongly recommend* the product or program to others.

In order for a product or program to succeed in the kids/youth marketplace it must meet the above Effectiveness Criteria. The degree to which it satisfies these criteria is the degree to which it is likely to succeed.

WHERE THE KIDS ARE

Central to any discussion on marketing to kids is an analysis of where a manufacturer or program developer/producer can expect to find and reach the kids he is targeting. While it may seem obvious where kids are, it is useful to break this out so that intelligent marketing approaches can be formulated. Kids are found, and can be reached, in any and all of the following five places.

1. AT HOME: At home kids can be reached primarily through television advertising, radio, computer programming and the Internet, and via kid publications as well as adult-targeted newspapers. Kids are also reached via product packaging that Mom brings home.

2. IN STORES: From babyhood, on, whether in strollers or in grocery carts or walking, kids are in stores—at first with their parents and later on alone. They are in grocery stores, drug stores, malls, convenience stores, toy stores, clothing stores, and just about every other kind of store imaginable. In these stores they are primarily reached via packaging. To a lesser extent they are reached through special displays, in-store videos, and audio tapes.

3. IN THE COMMUNITY: Out around town kids are in such locales as movie theaters, fast-food outlets, and sports facilities. Here kids are reached through packaging, promotions, film clips and film previews, movie theater displays, store signage, and sports posters and publications.

4. IN SCHOOLS: Before kindergarten a large percentage of the kid population are in day-care centers and other preschool programs. Here they are reached primarily via publications and television. From kindergarten on, kids are reached via publications, promotions, tie-ins, and giveaways related to kid-targeted products and programs.

5. IN AUTOMOBILES: Before kids can drive on their own they spend a great deal of time in the family car. Regular radio broadcasting can reach and appeal to young people increasingly as they get older. For the 3-through-14 set there are kids' radio stations such as Disney, Fox Kids radio and Radio AAHS, which is beaming its 24-hours-a-day children's programming in at least 27 cities in the United States.

MARKETING TO THE SUCCESSIVE AGE SEGMENTS VIA VARIOUS MEDIA

In this section we will look at the following pathways for appealing to kids: TV programming and advertising; packaging; promotions; magazines; newspapers; radio; computer programming; and the Internet. And given the distinct differences between the succeeding age segments as they are outlined in this book, namely birth-through-2, 3-through-7, 8-through-12, 13-through-15, and 16-through-19, each of these segments will be discussed separately in terms of which, if any, of the above modes reach and appeal to them.

THE BIRTH-THROUGH-2-YEAR-OLD

For obvious reasons, infants and toddlers are relatively limited in what they are able and ready to pay attention to and understand to the extent that they might communicate to their parents which things they want. Toward the older end of this target, however, as they near 3 years of age, children may be sufficiently influenced by what they see on television or in stores, e.g., toys that come in kid-targeted packaging, to generate requests. Or they may be sufficiently captivated by colorful and character-inhabited packaging in grocery-store aisles as they glide by in Mom's grocery cart. Specifically, marketing impacts this age group in the following ways.

TV PROGRAMMING AND ADVERTISING: Between the ages of birth through approximately the end of the first year of life, infants, while they might be entertained and distracted from time to time by television programming and advertising, will not comprehend enough of any message that is being delivered for it to have any real impact. By the second and third years of life, however—especially toward the end of the third year—children, through sustained exposure to certain TV stimuli such as *Sesame Street* characters or *Barney,* are likely to start identifying with these characters to the point of wanting them, and any other products being marketed, when they see them, e.g., on packaging or in a toy store. The same holds true for ads. As a result of sustained exposure, these toddlers may begin to make requests based upon what they have been watching.

PACKAGING: It's a similar story when it comes to packaging: negligible impact of packaging during the first year. At ages 2 and 3, however, children will respond to child-targeted packaging in stores or in print ads by pointing and gesturing and through communication, such as "Can I have that, Mommy?" Cereal boxes or kid-targeted snacks, for example, that have large and colorful animal characters on them will attract children more than boxes that do not have such child-friendly and kid-attracting visuals. *Jurassic Park* visuals, e.g., dinosaurs looming large on a cereal-box front panel, will certainly catch the attention of potential child consumers over tamer packaging without such visually conspicuous and involving visuals.

PROMOTIONS: Many promotions are too sophisticated for the birth-through-2-year-old to grasp, but there are others that do make an impact. Fast-food chains that promote the latest Warner Brothers (*Batman*) or Disney (*Hercules*) release, for example, use attractive and colorful themed packaging and the strong appeal of surprises and toys to maximum effect; 2-year-olds do not escape the impact of this appeal.

MAGAZINES AND BOOKS: Birth-through-2-year-olds have little contact with magazines. They do have, however, considerable exposure to books via their parents' and grandparents' reading to them. Exposure to characters in books, such as Barney or the Muppets or Disney characters, will begin to make its impact.

NEWSPAPERS: Virtually no impact.

RADIO: Very little impact. The audio medium requires an ability to attend that in most cases goes beyond the capacities of the birth-through-2 target child. Certain songs or chanted, sing-songy phrases may have an appeal to the older end of this age segment, however.

COMPUTER PROGRAMMING: Only during the third year of life can the most basic of "computer" systems be interacted with by the 2+ year-old. Sega's Pico Learning System is an example of a "computer" system that could have appeal at this young age. What the future holds that will match the abilities of this young child is left for us to discover.

Two-year-old-friendly, or even younger-targeted, technology may be developed that directly matches the capabilities and needs of the birth-through-2-year-old. Could you imagine child-friendly computer screens and a "mouse" (controls) in the crib? On a child's stroller?

Computer programming is included in a chapter on "Marketing to Kids" because the nature of the programming content—for example, featuring a popular character that is available for purchase, e.g., a stuffed animal—constitutes marketing. And certain computer programs directly market related products via their programming. *KidSoft* magazine, for example, directly markets its programs via a CD catalogue that is included with each issue.

THE INTERNET: Virtually no involvement or impact. But again, who knows what interfacing technology may evolve in the future?

THE 3-THROUGH-7-YEAR-OLD

Save for more sophisticated technological interfaces such as are required on the Internet and by adult-oriented newspapers, the average 3-through-7-year-old is fully ready and able to be impacted by most all forms of marketing media.

TV PROGRAMMING AND ADVERTISING: The 3-through-7-year-old is especially accepting of TV programming influence and TV advertising because he does not yet have the mature logical/rational skills of the 8-through-12-year-old. These young kids tend to accept things at face value. This is, therefore, a strong argument for responsibility in advertising when attempting to influence these young children. The 3-through-7-year-old is also highly visual in the way that he relates to the world. The left hemisphere of the cortex, which specializes among other things in verbal and linguistic capabilities, has not yet fully developed its linear and logical capacities, as it will in the next stage, 8 through 12.

What Works: Concrete, highly visual depictions of the product in use. For example, if you've a toy, what works is to show the toy being played with and enjoyed, especially focusing on the different fun features of the toy. Avoid abstract messages or complicated formats that require logic to "put together" or figure out. Slapstick humor, such as that utilized in the TV spots of Little Caesar's pizza, definitely works. The use of heroes/role models such as star sports figures also is a sure bet for the 3-through-7-year-old.

PACKAGING: Whether it's kids shopping on their own or Mom shopping with an eye for what her children are going to like, colorful, kid-targeted packaging has a strong role to play in marketing to the 3-through-7-year-old.

What Works: Bright colors—especially neons and bright reds, blues and yellows. Bold graphic designs which are not too abstract; characters that are strong, fun, popular, and attractive, and that are prominently displayed in characteristic and fun action poses. While "branding"—that is, the communication of the manufacturer's and brand's names on the packaging—is important to the manufacturer, it is not particularly important to the 3-through-7-year-old. The 3-through-7-year-old is primarily visual in his orientation to packaging and typically will not pay much attention to verbal information on packaging unless it's directly related to the "fun" visuals, e.g., a character's name underneath the character. To the extent that the product delivers strong play or fun or pleasure value for the 3-through-7-year-old, the prominent display of the product and its features is important as well. Ideally, if a character is utilized, that character should have a meaningful interaction/role with the product, such as dipping a cracker into a cheese snack or pulling apart the two halves of an Oreo cookie.

PROMOTIONS: The 3-through-7-year-old is also very open to promotions—whether it's a fast-food chain's tie-in with a feature film or a send-away for a toy gizmo or a free Halloween mask at the local toy store. Again, part of the reason for this lies in the fact that the critical/logical/rational mind is not yet fully developed. Children aged 3 through 7 tend not to be too critical of promotional items directed at them; in a sense they "want it all." They are more interested in accumulating and having "lots of stuff" than in discriminating between things being offered to them.

MAGAZINES: Toward the top end of the 3-through-7-year range, children typically begin to read magazines directed toward kids, such as *Disney Adventures* magazine or *Boys' Life* or *Scholastic.*

NEWSPAPERS: Very little involvement with newspapers for the 3-through-7-year-old; some comics reading.

RADIO: Where there are children's radio stations, and on those occasions when Mom or Dad tunes them in or when 5-, 6-, or 7-year-olds ask for them to be tuned in, there is some access via radio to kids toward the top end of the 3-through-7-year age spread. The appearance of radio stations wholly or in part dedicated to children's programming is on the upswing. The current dominant "players" in this arena are Radio AAHS, Disney, and Fox.

COMPUTER PROGRAMMING: Computer programs that feature popular characters naturally lead to the reinforcement of interest in those characters as they appear on other products and programs. There are also some programs that contain advertisements that cross-sell other line items. The 3-through-7-year-old is an appropriate target for this type of marketing.

THE INTERNET: While a growing number of kids toward the top end of this 3-through-7 segment are becoming involved in the Internet— especially with kid-targeted web sites—most Internet activity doesn't really begin until the next developmental stage, ages 8 through 12.

THE 8-THROUGH-12-YEAR-OLD

TV PROGRAMMING AND ADVERTISING: The 1996 *Roper Youth Report*[1] indicates that American boys and girls ages 8 through 12 are watching an average of almost 30 hours of television each week. Given the degree of interest and attention that these young people are investing in TV viewing, and given the dynamic impact that strong visual presentations can have—with their fast pacing, bright colors, characters, MTV-like quick cuts, and special effects—the impact of this viewing of programming and TV ads is substantial. The millions of dollars spent by kid-targeting companies on TV advertising attests to this dynamic impact.

The 8-through-12-year-old TV viewer, however, is quite different from what he was when he was in the 3-through-7 developmental stage. This older TV watcher is:

More Discriminating: Given the evolution of his logical and rational capabilities via this stage's focus on left-brain development, this 8-through-12-year-old is more able to analyze what is being presented and to weigh its promises. He is also more able to compare and contrast what is being offered with his picture of reality, that is, what has been delivered in the past on such promises. He is less impulsive and far more reflective in his learning skills.

More Reality-Oriented: Whereas in the previous 3-through-7 stage she was more fantasy-oriented and more accepting of anything and everything as being possible, the 8-through-12-year-old is now more realistic. TV ads, for example, that use quite childish fantasy elements such as simple magic and youngish characters may be considered to be "beneath" this more sophisticated 8-through-12-year-old.

There are exceptions, however. Certain apparently youngish-looking characters such as the Trix Rabbit or Mickey Mouse can effectively appeal to this 8-through-12-year-old because (a) He is seeing or watching them in the privacy and safety of his home, away from the judgmental eyes of his peers, and (b) these characters nostalgically appeal to the "child within" this trying-to-grow-up-and-be-older child.

More Cognitively Sophisticated: This older 8-through-12-year-old, because of his more advanced cognitive abilities, is necessarily more able to respond to increased abstraction—in fact he prefers it. This translates to, among other things, a preference for more abstract visuals, more complicated verbal messages (they still need to be comprehensible), and more abstract humor.

What Works: In addition to what is implied above, what works in TV advertising that targets the 8-through-12-year-old is the use of relatively quick pacing, both slapstick and more abstract humor, and both realistic and heroic role models. If real children are utilized in the ads, care should be taken to make them at least slightly older than the 8-through-12 target, i.e., 12-, 13-, and 14-year-olds and older. Should the 8-through-12-year-old experience such stimuli as visuals, characters, and real children that he perceives as "too young," the conclusion that he will typically come to is "This is not for me" or "This is for younger kids." The marketing goal is "like-me" associations with kids of the target child's own age and upward "emulation" associations.

PACKAGING: More often than not marketers are targeting broad age ranges of children, i.e., 4-through-12-year-olds, rather than just targeting 8-through-12-year-olds. If marketers were to target only 8-through-12-year-olds, there would be substantial differences in approaches to packaging.

Graphics: Graphics typically would be more abstract—i.e., with more angularity of lines and more complexity rather than the rounder, softer, simpler, more concrete lines that appeal to a younger child. Symbols, if utilized, would be more sophisticated for this age group.

Colors: The packaging approach to coloration would be less primary in nature and more toward bright neon-like colors and more complex color combinations. For this age range, there is often in fact a "not-for-me" backlash against primary colors as being too babyish.

Characters: Characters, if utilized, are not simple, childish cartoon characters and are more often realistic and more complex, i.e., real people such as sports heroes. If they are "cartoonized" characters, they would be more abstractly drawn, more "edgy" characters, or would have sophisticated Content elements like the Simpsons, or the round yet personality-deep M&M's characters we see in that candy's TV ads.

Verbal Increase: While the 8-through-12-year-old is still primarily visual in his approach to marketing messages, he is now cognitively able to decipher and appreciate verbal messages and details that earlier he would not have related to.

PROMOTIONS: The 8-through-12-year-old is a strong target for appropriate promotional efforts. This group's evolving egos/identities thrive on attention from outside the family world. This age child is beginning to enter the mainstream of society and an expression of this is his increased communications/interactions via mail, phone, and computer, and increased involvement in clubs and organizations.

MAGAZINES: The 8-through-12-year-old is also much more likely to be subscribing to and reading magazines. Among the most popular of these are electronic gaming magazines such as *Nintendo Power, Sports Illustrated for Kids, TV Guide, National Geographic World, Nickelodeon Magazine, Scholastic* magazine (which is distributed through schools), and *Disney Adventures: The Magazine for Kids.* This successful lineup of publications directly reflects the interests and activities of the 8-through-12-year-old: sports, clubs and organizations, learning, and entertainment/fun.

A little-known fact about the *way* in which 8-through-12-year-olds and older kids read is very important to keep in mind for marketers who are considering spending advertising dollars on publications. Whereas adults tend to skip around in their reading of a publication, seeking out only those articles and ads which have the most pertinence to them, 8+ year-olds tend to read their magazines cover to cover, paying attention to everything offered. Part of the reason for this is that kids of this age are not as future-oriented as older teens and adults. Kids for the most part are not concerned about whatever might be next on their day's agenda, and are freed up to be in the present and pay longer and closer attention to what they are reading.

NEWSPAPERS: Newspaper reading begins during this 8-through-12 stage for a segment of this target population, but is typically limited to kid-oriented sections such as the comic section. There are a few metropolitan newspapers which have a dedicated section for kids; this increases 8-through-12 readership and represents a realistic opportunity for marketers.

RADIO: According to Roper Starch, almost 90 percent of children 8 through 12 listen to the radio from one to sixteen hours a week. Where there are dedicated children's radio stations such as in the cities served by Disney, Fox, or Radio AAHS, many are the 8-through-12-year-olds who will tune in. For the most part, however, the 8-through-12-year-old is already listening to young-adult–targeted music stations.

COMPUTER PROGRAMMING: Why would computer programming be listed as a way to reach kids with advertising and marketing efforts? There are two reasons. The first is that certain properties—licensed characters such as Disney or Warner Brothers characters—may be used in educational programming, thus promoting them in the eyes of young customers. The second reason is that certain programs such as the CD catalogue that accompanies editions of *KidSoft* magazine directly advertise software. No doubt we will see more and more direct advertising and promotion via software programming itself.

THE INTERNET: A growing number of children 8 through 12 are accessing on-line services on a frequent basis (approximately 20 percent according to Roper, slightly more males than females). This number increases as children grow into their teens and will certainly increase as more and more children acquire access to the Internet and as its options for kids proliferate. Advertising and marketing directly to these Internet users and browsers, therefore, is a solid opportunity and one that is only destined to expand over time.

THE 13-THROUGH-15-YEAR-OLD

In terms of how to reach the 13-through-15-year-old and the parameters for doing so, there is not much qualitatively different that should be included in your approach via the media as they have been listed: TV programming and advertising, promotions, magazines, newspapers, radio, computer programming, and the Internet. In other words, the 13-through-15-year-old is similar to the 8-through-12-year-old in the types of media used to reach them and in preferences for their presentation. One exception to this is packaging that is directly targeted to and designed for kids in that it uses kid titles for the brand, young kid-appealing characters, and kid-appealing graphics. The typical 13-through-15-year-old perceives himself as "no longer a kid" and therefore any advertising or promotions directly naming "kids" as their target or communicating "kid" through visual means are likely to be deemed "not for me" and "for younger kids."

Among the different mediums, slight differences quantitatively are present. Newspaper readership and use of the Internet, for example, are slightly more prevalent among this age of older youth.

THE 16-THROUGH-19-YEAR-OLD

With the family car keys or his own car keys in his hands representing greatly increased mobility and independence, and with his eye toward his future as an adult, the 16-through-19-year-old, for all practical marketing purposes, is more like an adult than a kid. He is going to seek out and prefer, therefore, primarily adult approaches to marketing such as those listed below.

> **TV PROGRAMMING AND ADVERTISING:** This late teen/young adult is going to prefer teen- and young-adult-targeted TV programming in terms of sitcoms, movies, prime-time dramas, game shows, and cable shows directly targeted at him, like MTV and other music programming.

> **PACKAGING AND PROMOTIONS:** Essentially adult in their approach.

> **MAGAZINES:** Adult and young-adult magazines.

NEWSPAPERS: Increased readership as the 16+ year-old matures into adulthood.

RADIO: Music, music, music—most of which is mainstream youth-targeted, i.e., Rock 'n' Roll, pop, rap and western.

COMPUTER PROGRAMMING AND USE OF THE INTERNET: Increased use of computer programming and on-line activity.

CHILD RESEARCH

No chapter on marketing to kids would be complete without a discussion of primary research, both qualitative and quantitative. Whether you are preparing quantitative or qualitative research, there are a number of pitfalls to avoid, based on our experience at YMS Consulting and on child-development principles. The major ones are these.

NOT TESTING AT ALL. Enough said.

TESTING FOR THE WRONG THINGS: At YMS, for example, when we prepare a qualitative test we do not call it a "focus group" but instead refer to it as "Subject Testing." The reason for this is that we use child-development information, past experience, and a thorough analysis of the product or program under study to develop a series of hypotheses about which aspects or attributes of the product or program to test for. These hypotheses include our predictions of how children are going to respond developmentally. Through careful analysis—before the test—we can eliminate much of what is irrelevant to test for and can then zero in on the really pertinent aspects of the project.

INADEQUATE STIMULI: A second pitfall when preparing test materials is using stimuli that are for one reason or another inadequate. To prepare stimuli correctly, keep the following in mind: (a) Keep the number of stimuli small and organized as much as you can around dichotomous choices—"Do you like this or that?"—especially for kids below the age of 8; (b) Make sure that competing stimuli are as equal as possible, e.g., in color, size, number of visual and verbal elements, etc.; (c) Whenever possible, provide three-dimensional objects rather than flat art.

USING TOO MANY WORDS: Children, especially below the age of 7 or 8, are extremely visual in their orientation to the world. A research pitfall is to rely too much on verbal explanations of concepts or on the verbal responses of kids. The recommendation is to utilize primarily visual approaches to stimuli and to ask children to interact with those visual elements directly—for example "Point at the part of the product you like best" or "Touch the part of the package you like the least."

BIASING CHILD RESPONDENTS: Avoiding bias in respondent responses is always a concern whether you are testing adults or kids. Kids, however, are particularly vulnerable to being swayed in their opinions by strong leaders, and these may emerge in subject test/focus groups. One approach to avoiding bias is to use silent voting techniques, such as having children whisper their responses in the moderator's ear or to have them "finger vote" behind their backs and out of sight of others, using one finger to indicate a particular preference, two fingers for another, and so forth.

NEGLECTING THE INTANGIBLES: A final pitfall—especially in qualitative testing—is to neglect the intangibles such as the child's energy level that is apparent in his response, his nonverbal and body cues that show his interest, or lack of interest, and his tone of voice. Many times these intangibles are as important as, or more important than, the voting tallies themselves. In the early 1980s Mattel Incorporated asked us to evaluate a new action-figure product line for boys that they were about to come out with called "He-Man." When we tested it with young boys, their energy and excitement level was so high that they literally ran across the room to play with the He-Man toys and it was difficult to pry them out of their eager hands when the test was over. *That's* high energy.

SUMMARY

By way of summarizing this chapter on successful marketing to kids, the following guidelines are presented to keep in front of you, no matter what medium you use as you attempt to reach and impact kids.

KIDS ARE PRIMARILY VISUAL: Especially below the age of 7, but even afterward, kids are primarily visual in their approach to ads, packaging, and promotional materials. Minimize the verbal and maximize the visual when targeting kids 12 and under.

KIDS ARE EMULATORY: Kids look to older kids, older characters, teens, and adults for their models and sources of emulation. As soon as elements in an ad or on packaging appear to be "too young" or the wrong gender, an immediate response of "This is not for me" can, and typically does, form.

KIDS ARE ACCUMULATORS: Especially below the age of 8, kids are very interested in getting "lots of stuff." Quantity is more important than quality for the younger child. After age 8, children are more quality-oriented and more serious collectors, but they still respond to offers of "lots of stuff."

KIDS LOVE SURPRISES: Whether it's a hidden toy inside a package, or a special effect in a TV ad, children love the excitement and extra payoff inherent in unexpected rewards and surprises.

KIDS LOVE WHAT'S NEW AND DIFFERENT: In certain categories kids are perhaps the most fickle of consumers. They can tire very quickly of certain kinds of products and programs. The implication is to constantly "freshen" your product lines and program lineups to cater to this desire for the new. Mattel's Barbie® line is the ultimate example of a line of products that is constantly and expertly being "freshened," added on to, and changed to keep it "new" in the eyes and hearts of its young female customers. There are a few exceptions to this rule. For example, kids (especially younger kids in some cases) will tend to love watching the same entertaining advertisement or video, or playing the same video game, over and over—at least until it is mastered.

BOYS EMULATE BOYS, GIRLS EMULATE BOYS AND GIRLS: It's common knowledge among marketers that for products and programs that are dual-gender in their targeting, girls will typically accept and enjoy boy characters, spokespersons, and child models and actors, but boys can be turned off by the use of female characters and actors and can quickly formulate the perception that "this is for girls."

As can be seen from the above discussions on marketing approaches to each of the different age groups, marketing to kids is a very segmented affair. Given the vast differences between a baby and a 19-year-old, today's marketer needs to constantly be aware of exactly who his target is and how to most appropriately and powerfully impact that target. Far too often management issues a decree to, for example, target 4-through-12-year-olds with a given product or program. Tricky business. There are many products that cannot bridge such an age gap, given the nature of what they are. Other products might be able to make the bridge, but one must be extremely careful in one's approach to such an objective.

CHAPTER 12

IN CONCLUSION

The successful creation, development, and marketing of products and programs to kids and young people from birth through 19 years of age—and their parents—depends upon a thorough understanding of females and males as they progress through each of the developmental stages.

Understanding kids at each stage means understanding their:

Capabilities
Perceptions
Motivations
Needs
Wants
Likes and dislikes

It also means understanding the needs, motivations, and wants of those children's parents—particularly Moms, when they are the primary purchasers.

And it doesn't stop there. There are actually three key pieces to the "success puzzle" when it comes to the effective creation, development, and marketing of a product, line of products, or program to a kid-targeted audience: *People* as the intended target, and this includes parents or other potential purchasers when they are involved; the *Product or Program* itself; and the *Marketplace*. The relationship between these three is shown in Figure 12.1.

PEOPLE

The most fundamental ingredient of success is a thorough understanding of your target audience: boys, girls, Moms, Dads—whoever is directly involved with the purchase and use of the item in question. How old are they? What do they want?

FIGURE 12.1

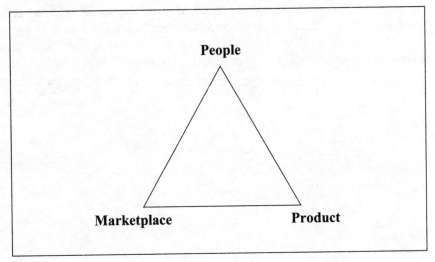

PRODUCT

It's critical to understand your product or program. What is its essence? What are its key features or attributes? What does it promise? What does it deliver? What is its payoff—what needs and wants does it satisfy? What are its key strengths? Its weaknesses?

MARKETPLACE

It's extremely important to know the marketplace into which your product or program is entering. What is the competition? What are the strengths and weaknesses of that competition? What are consumer perceptions regarding the competition? What are trade perceptions regarding the product or program category and regarding your product or program? What is your product's point of difference from competing items—what makes your product unique? How does your pricing structure compare to that of competing items? What should you know about the idiosyncrasies of distribution and retailing for your particular product or program?

While the above may sound like a basic college course called "Product Development/Marketing 101," it can't be emphasized enough that one must continually look at the "big picture" of People, Product, and Marketplace in order to have a fighting chance in today's competitive business world.

In *What Kids Buy and Why,* it has been our emphasis to focus on the "people" aspect of the equation. So many child-targeting product developers and marketers tend to toss *all* kids willy-nilly into a single basket labeled "kids." The central thrust and intent of this book has been to "get up underneath" each of the age segments of today's boys and girls, to provide you with the in-depth understanding that is needed to succeed in the kid marketplace. We enjoyed the ride, and we hope you did as well.

Notes

INTRODUCTION

1. JAMES MCNEAL, *Kids as Customers* (New York: Lexington Books, 1992).
2. International Quality and Productivity Center, 150 Clove Road, Little Falls, NJ 07424-0401. Telephone (800) 882-8684.
3. Institute for International Research, 708 Third Avenue, New York, NY 10017-4103. Telephone (212) 261-3500.
4. *Marketing to Kids Report,* 3364 Country Rose Circle, Encinitas, CA 22024-5709. Telephone (619) 756-6446.
5. *Selling to Kids,* published bimonthly by Phillips Business Information, 7313 Park Heights Ave., Ste. 201, Baltimore, MD 21208. Telephone (410) 764-6525.

CHAPTER 1: A WINNING FORMULA

1. T. BERRY BRAZELTON, "Early Intervention: What Does It Mean?" in Hiram Fitzgerald, B. M. Lester, and M. Yogman, *Theory and Research in Behavioral Pediatrics,* vol. I (New York: Plenum Publishing Corp., 1982).
2. HERMAN T. EPSTEIN, "Brain Growth Spurts," *On the Beam: New Horizons for Learning,* I, no. 2 (April 1981).
3. ERIK ERIKSON, *Childhood and Society* (New York: W. W. Norton & Company, 1964).
4. MICHAEL S. GAZZANIGA, *Mind Matters: How Mind and Brain Interact to Create Our Conscious Lives* (Boston: Houghton Mifflin Company, 1988).
5. JOHN HERMAN, "Dreaming Affected by Daytime Experience," *Brain Mind Bulletin* Themepak No. 9.
6. LAWRENCE KOHLBERG, *Moral Stages and the Idea of Justice,* vol. 1 in Kohlberg, *The Philosophy of Moral Development* (New York: HarperCollins, 1981).
7. PAUL D. MACLEAN, *The Triune Brain in Evolution* (New York: Plenum Publishing Corp., 1990).
8. JOSEPH CHILTON PEARCE, *Evolution's End* (HarperSan Francisco, 1992).
9. JEAN PIAGET, *The Origins of Intelligence in Children* (Madison, CT: International Universities Press, Inc., 1992).
10. HOWARD GARDNER, *Frames of Mind* (New York: Basic Books, 1985).
11. PIAGET, *The Origins of Intelligence in Children.*
12. ERIKSON, *Childhood and Society.*
13. KOHLBERG, *Moral Stages and the Idea of Justice.*
14. PEARCE, *Evolution's End.*
15. KEN WILBER, *The Spectrum of Consciousness* (Wheaton, IL: Quest Books, 1993).

CHAPTER 2: KID EMPOWERMENT

1. STEPHEN VINCENT BENET, *John Brown's Body* (Cutchogue, NY: Buccaneer Books, 1996).
2. JANE HEALEY, *Endangered Minds* (New York: Touchstone/Simon & Schuster, 1990), p. 226.

CHAPTER 4: BIRTH THROUGH AGE 2

1. JOSEPH CHILTON PEARCE, *The Magical Child* (New York: E. P. Dutton, 1977).
2. PATRICIA MARKS GREENFIELD, *Mind and Media: The Effects of Television, Video Games, and Computers* (Cambridge, MA: Harvard University Press, 1984).
3. ANTONIO DAMASIO, *Descartes' Error: Emotion, Reasoning and the Human Brain* (New York: Grosset/Putnam, 1994).
4. GREENFIELD, *Mind and Media.*
5. DAMASIO, *Descartes' Error.*
6. DANIEL GOLEMAN, *Emotional Intelligence* (New York: Bantam, 1995).
7. JOSEPH LEDOUX, *The Emotional Brain* (New York: Simon & Schuster, 1996).
8. HOWARD GARDNER, *Multiple Intelligences: The Theory in Practice* (New York: Basic Books, 1993).
9. PEARCE, *The Magical Child.*
10. GOLEMAN, *Emotional Intelligence.*
11. PEARCE, *The Magical Child.*

CHAPTER 5: AGES 3 THROUGH 7

1. GEORGE SANTAYANA, *Dialogues in Limbo with Three New Dialogues* (New York: Kelley, 1926).
2. JOSEPH CHILTON PEARCE, *Evolution's End* (HarperSan Francisco, 1992); Jean Piaget, *The Origins of Intelligence in Children* (Madison, CT: International Universities Press, Inc., 1992).
3. PEARCE, *Evolution's End.*
4. LAWRENCE KOHLBERG, *Moral Stages and the Idea of Justice,* vol. 1 in Kohlberg, *The Philosophy of Moral Development* (New York: HarperCollins, 1981).

CHAPTER 6: AGES 8 THROUGH 12

1. JAMES BALDWIN, *Nobody Knows My Name* (New York: Dial Press, 1961).
2. JOSEPH CHILTON PEARCE, *Evolution's End* (HarperSan Francisco, 1992).
3. Ibid.
4. JEAN PIAGET, *The Origins of Intelligence in Children* (Madison, CT: International Universities Press, Inc., 1992).
5. DOUGLAS RUSHKOFF, *Playing the Future: How Kids' Culture Can Teach Us to Thrive in an Age of Chaos* (New York: HarperCollins, 1996).

CHAPTER 7: AGES 13 THROUGH 15

1. LOGAN SMITH, *Afterthoughts* (Boston: Houghton Mifflin Company, 1984).

CHAPTER 8: AGES 16 THROUGH 19

1. JOHN KEATS, *Endymion* (New York: Odyssey Press, 1935).
2. JOSEPH CHILTON PEARCE, *Evolution's End* (HarperSan Francisco, 1992), pp. 138–142.
3. ADRIAN RAINE, "Low Arousal and the Life of Crime," *American Journal of Psychiatry,* November 1995.
4. HERMAN T. EPSTEIN, "Brain Growth Spurts," *On the Beam: New Horizons for Learning,* I, no. 2 (April 1981).
5. JEAN PIAGET, *The Origins of Intelligence in Children* (Madison, CT: International Universities Press, 1992).

CHAPTER 9: GENDER DIFFERENCES: BARBIE® MEETS GODZILLA®

1. JOHN GRAY, PH.D., *Men, Women and Relationships* (New York: Harper Paperbacks, 1993).
2. LINDA BRANNON, *Gender: Psychological Perspectives* (Needham, MA: Allyn & Bacon, 1996).

INDEX